The Positive Power of the Internet

and Social Media

Celebrating the Positive Impact of the Internet and Social Media.

Contents

Introduction: The Positive Power of the Internet and Social Media

The Internet and social media have revolutionized the way we live, work, communicate, and connect. In less than three decades, they have transformed from niche technologies to global tools that shape every aspect of modern life. While much has been written about the dangers of digital platforms, such as cyberbullying, privacy concerns, and addiction, this book takes a different approach: celebrating the positive impact of the Internet and social media.

In a world where over 5 billion people are connected to the Internet, and 4.8 billion actively use social media, these platforms have become essential parts of daily life. Social media has democratized communication, allowing anyone with a smartphone or computer to share their thoughts, ideas, and experiences with the world. It has given a voice to the voiceless, created opportunities for businesses, and fostered communities that transcend geographical borders. The Internet has made knowledge more accessible than ever before, transforming education, science, business, and culture on a global scale.

A New Era of Global Connectivity

One of the most powerful aspects of the Internet is its ability to connect people across continents, bridging cultures, languages, and ideologies. Social media platforms like Facebook, Instagram, Twitter, and TikTok have amplified this connectivity, enabling individuals to communicate in real-time with anyone, anywhere. These connections have made the world feel smaller and more interconnected, allowing people to build relationships, share experiences, and learn from each other in ways that were unimaginable just a few decades ago.

For families separated by distance, social media offers a lifeline of communication. For businesses, it provides a direct channel to reach customers across the globe. For individuals, it serves as a platform to express opinions, showcase talents, or advocate for causes they believe in. The global village that the Internet and social media have created is fostering a new era of collaboration, empathy, and shared knowledge.

The Democratization of Information

Before the Internet, access to information was often limited by geography, financial resources, or institutional gatekeepers. Libraries, universities, and media outlets-controlled knowledge, and individuals had limited means of contributing to or distributing information on a large scale. The rise of the Internet has democratized information, breaking down barriers and making knowledge accessible to anyone with an Internet connection.

Platforms like Wikipedia, YouTube, and Reddit have emerged as hubs of knowledge, offering everything from academic papers and tutorials to personal experiences and expert advice. Social media, in particular, has become a tool for knowledge sharing, where communities can come together to discuss everything from niche hobbies to pressing global issues. This newfound accessibility has empowered people to educate themselves, develop skills, and engage in lifelong learning - without the need for formal institutions.

Empowering Voices and Social Change

Social media has not only connected people, but it has also empowered individuals and communities to advocate for change. Movements such as #MeToo, Black Lives Matter, and Fridays for Future gained global traction through social media, using platforms like Twitter and Instagram to spread their message, mobilize supporters, and demand justice. By amplifying underrepresented voices, social media has transformed from a tool for social interaction into a powerful instrument for social change.

This digital activism has led to real-world consequences. Governments, corporations, and institutions have been forced to respond to public pressure brought about by online movements. Social media has given power to ordinary individuals, allowing them to hold those in authority accountable and to push for change on issues such as gender equality, racial justice, climate action, and human rights.

Catalysing Innovation and Economic Growth

The Internet and social media have transformed the global economy, creating new industries and opportunities for individuals and businesses alike. Small businesses, entrepreneurs, and creators can now reach global audiences through digital platforms, bypassing traditional gatekeepers such as brick-and-mortar stores or media outlets. Social media has become a marketplace for creativity and entrepreneurship, where ideas can be tested, products launched, and brands built with minimal upfront costs.

Moreover, platforms like LinkedIn and professional communities have redefined the concept of networking. Individuals can connect with mentors, partners, or employers across the globe, expanding career opportunities in ways that were once impossible. Social media has also become a space for learning and professional development, with access to courses, webinars, and industry-specific knowledge, allowing people to continuously upgrade their skills.

Fostering a Cultural Renaissance

The Internet and social media have sparked a renaissance in creativity and self-expression. No longer confined to traditional media outlets, artists, musicians, writers, and filmmakers can share their work directly with global audiences. Platforms like YouTube, Instagram, and TikTok have empowered creators to bypass industry gatekeepers, giving rise to independent creators who have built careers entirely online.

This cultural revolution has allowed diverse voices to emerge and thrive. The global reach of social media has facilitated cross-cultural exchanges, where artists from different backgrounds collaborate, share influences, and bring together distinct cultural elements in new and innovative ways. This has not only enriched global culture but has also provided visibility to underrepresented communities and marginalized groups whose voices were often silenced by traditional media.

Building Communities and Support Systems

One of the most heartening aspects of social media is its ability to build supportive communities. From forums focused on niche hobbies to support groups for people facing mental health challenges, the Internet offers spaces where individuals can find belonging and camaraderie. For those dealing with isolation, illness, or difficult life circumstances, these online communities provide much-needed connection, advice, and encouragement.

In times of crisis, social media has also proven to be an invaluable tool for organizing relief efforts and providing real-time information. Whether coordinating aid during natural disasters or offering support during the COVID-19 pandemic, social platforms have facilitated collaboration between individuals, organizations, and governments.

A Balanced Perspective

While it is crucial to acknowledge the challenges and potential harms associated with the Internet and social media, it is equally important to recognize their potential for good. The rapid pace of technological change has brought with it profound shifts in how we live, work, and interact. By focusing on the positive impacts of these digital platforms, this book seeks to highlight the ways in which the Internet and social media have enriched lives, empowered individuals, and transformed society.

As we delve into the various dimensions of the Internet's and social media's positive impact - from business and education to culture and social justice - this book will provide a comprehensive look at how these tools can continue to be a force for progress in the years to come.

Next, we will move on to **Chapter 1: Revolutionizing Communication and Global Connectivity**, where we explore how social media has redefined the way we connect with each other and the world.

Chapter 1: Revolutionizing Communication and Global Connectivity

1.1 The Evolution of Communication

Communication has undergone a remarkable transformation over the centuries. From the early days of handwritten letters and carrier pigeons to the advent of telegraphs and telephones, each technological advancement has redefined how we connect with others. The most recent leap in this evolution is the Internet, which has brought about a paradigm shift in the way we communicate, breaking down barriers of distance and time.

The early Internet, with its email systems and bulletin board services, set the stage for a new era of digital communication. The introduction of social media platforms marked a significant turning point, as these platforms allowed for real-time, interactive communication on a global scale. Social media has not only enhanced personal communication but has also transformed professional interactions, political discourse, and public engagement.

1.2 The Global Reach of Social Media

Social media platforms like Facebook, Twitter, Instagram, and TikTok have created a new form of global interconnectivity. These platforms enable individuals to connect with others across continents instantly, facilitating communication that was once impossible. Here's how social media has expanded our global reach:

- **Instant Connectivity:** Social media allows users to connect with friends, family, and colleagues around the world in real-time. Whether it's a video call with a relative overseas or a chat with a colleague in a different country, social media has made instant communication a reality.

- **Global Networks:** Social media platforms enable users to build global networks of contacts and collaborators. Professionals can connect with peers and industry leaders from various countries, while individuals can join communities that share their interests, regardless of geographic location.

- **Cultural Exchange:** Social media facilitates the exchange of cultural ideas, traditions, and experiences. Users can share aspects of their culture and learn about others, fostering greater understanding and appreciation across different cultures.

1.3 Breaking Down Geographical Barriers

One of the most significant impacts of social media is its ability to transcend geographical boundaries. This has led to numerous benefits:

- **Enhanced Collaboration:** Social media tools and platforms enable international collaboration on projects, research, and initiatives. Professionals from different countries can work together seamlessly, sharing information and resources without the constraints of physical distance.

- **Virtual Communities:** Online forums and social media groups allow individuals to find and connect with others who share their interests, even if they are located far apart. These virtual communities offer support, advice, and camaraderie, creating a sense of belonging that might otherwise be difficult to find.

- **Real-Time Updates:** Social media provides real-time updates on global events, from breaking news to live broadcasts. This immediacy helps people stay informed about developments around the world and participate in global conversations.

1.4 Social Media in Crisis Communication

During times of crisis, social media has proven to be an invaluable tool for communication:

- **Emergency Alerts:** Social media platforms are used to disseminate emergency alerts and updates quickly. Governments, organizations, and individuals can share critical information about natural disasters, health emergencies, and other crises in real-time.

- **Coordination of Relief Efforts:** Social media helps coordinate relief efforts by connecting volunteers, organizations, and affected individuals. During natural disasters or humanitarian crises, social media can facilitate the organization of aid and resources.

- **Support Networks:** In times of personal or community crises, social media provides a platform for people to offer and receive support. Online communities can come together to provide emotional support, practical help, and financial assistance.

1.5 Social Media and Personal Relationships

Social media has transformed personal relationships in various ways:

- **Maintaining Connections:** Social media platforms make it easier to stay in touch with friends and family members, regardless of distance. Sharing updates, photos, and messages helps maintain connections that might otherwise dwindle.

- **Reconnecting with Old Friends:** Social media makes it possible to reconnect with people from the past, such as old classmates or former colleagues. These platforms provide tools to search for and reach out to individuals who were once significant in one's life.

- **Enhancing Relationships:** Social media can enhance personal relationships by providing new ways to interact. Users can engage with each other through comments, likes, and shares, creating opportunities for deeper connections and shared experiences.

1.6 Social Media in Professional Contexts

The impact of social media extends beyond personal relationships into professional contexts:

- **Networking Opportunities:** Social media platforms like LinkedIn have revolutionized professional networking. Users can connect with industry peers, potential employers, and business partners, expanding their professional circles and opportunities.

- **Professional Development:** Social media provides access to professional development resources, including webinars, industry news, and thought leadership articles. This access helps individuals stay informed about trends and advancements in their fields.

- **Recruitment and Job Search:** Employers and job seekers use social media to find and fill job openings. Recruiters can identify potential candidates, while job seekers can discover opportunities and showcase their skills and achievements.

1.7 The Future of Communication and Connectivity

As technology continues to evolve, so will the ways we communicate and connect:

- **Advancements in Technology:** Emerging technologies such as 5G, augmented reality (AR), and virtual reality (VR) will further enhance communication and connectivity. These technologies promise to create more immersive and interactive experiences.

- **Increased Integration:** Social media platforms will continue to integrate with other technologies, such as smart devices and IoT (Internet of Things), leading to new forms of communication and interaction.

- **Global Challenges:** While social media offers numerous benefits, it also presents challenges, including privacy concerns and digital divide issues. Addressing these challenges will be crucial in ensuring that the positive impacts of social media continue to be realized.

Conclusion

Social media has revolutionized communication and global connectivity in profound ways. By breaking down geographical barriers, facilitating real-time interaction, and enabling global networks, social media has transformed how we connect with each other and the world. As we continue to navigate this digital landscape, it is essential to recognize and harness the positive power of these platforms while addressing the challenges they may present.

In the next chapter, **Chapter 2: Amplifying Voices and Supporting Social Movements**, we will explore how social media has become a powerful tool for advocacy, social change, and community empowerment.

Chapter 2: Amplifying Voices and Supporting Social Movements

2.1 The Role of Social Media in Advocacy

Social media has emerged as a critical tool for advocacy, offering individuals and organizations new ways to raise awareness, mobilize supporters, and drive change. Unlike traditional media, which often involves lengthy processes and significant resources, social media provides a platform for instant, widespread communication and engagement.

Key aspects of social media's role in advocacy include:

- **Direct Communication:** Social media allows advocates to communicate directly with their audience, bypassing traditional media channels. This direct line of communication helps to disseminate messages quickly and engage with supporters on a personal level.

- **Grassroots Mobilization:** Social media has enabled grassroots movements to flourish by providing a platform for organizing, fundraising, and rallying support. Activists can leverage the reach of social media to build momentum and mobilize large numbers of people around a cause.

- **Real-Time Updates:** Social media provides real-time updates and instant feedback, allowing advocates to respond to developments quickly and adjust their strategies as needed.

2.2 Notable Social Movements Powered by Social Media

Several high-profile social movements have harnessed the power of social media to effect change:

- **#MeToo Movement:** The #MeToo movement, which began as a hashtag on Twitter, has become a global phenomenon advocating against sexual harassment and assault. By sharing personal experiences and supporting one another, individuals have brought attention to systemic issues of abuse and inequality in various industries.

- **Black Lives Matter (BLM):** The Black Lives Matter movement uses social media to highlight issues of racial injustice and police violence. Through viral hashtags, online petitions, and mobilisation efforts, BLM has catalysed global protests and discussions about systemic racism.

- **Fridays for Future:** Inspired by Greta Thunberg's solo climate strike, Fridays for Future leverages social media to mobilize young people worldwide in the fight against climate change. The movement has organized global strikes, raised awareness about environmental issues, and pressured policymakers to take action.

2.3 The Impact of Social Media on Social Justice

Social media has had a profound impact on social justice by amplifying marginalized voices and bringing attention to important issues:

- **Visibility and Representation:** Social media provides a platform for marginalized communities to share their experiences and perspectives, increasing visibility and representation. This has led to greater awareness of issues affecting these communities and has facilitated discussions about systemic inequalities.

- **Accountability and Transparency:** Social media plays a role in holding institutions and individuals accountable for their actions. By sharing evidence of injustice and mobilizing public opinion, social media can prompt investigations, policy changes, and reforms.

- **Community Support:** Social media fosters community support and solidarity, allowing individuals to connect with others who share their experiences and concerns. This sense of community can be empowering and provide a foundation for collective action.

2.4 Strategies for Effective Social Media Advocacy

To effectively harness the power of social media for advocacy, it is important to employ strategic approaches:

- **Crafting a Clear Message:** A clear and compelling message is crucial for engaging supporters and driving action. Advocates should focus on creating concise, impactful content that resonates with their audience.

- **Building a Community:** Engaging with followers and building a supportive community can amplify the reach of advocacy efforts. Responding to comments, sharing user-generated content, and fostering dialogue can strengthen relationships and increase engagement.

- **Utilizing Multiple Platforms:** Different social media platforms offer unique features and audiences. Advocates can utilize a range of platforms to reach diverse demographics and maximize their impact.

- **Leveraging Visual Content:** Visual content, such as images and videos, often has a higher engagement rate than text alone. Utilizing compelling visuals can capture attention and convey messages more effectively.

2.5 Challenges and Considerations in Social Media Advocacy

While social media offers powerful tools for advocacy, there are challenges and considerations to keep in mind:

- **Misinformation and Disinformation:** The rapid spread of misinformation and disinformation on social media can undermine advocacy efforts and create confusion. Advocates should prioritize fact-checking and provide accurate information to counter false narratives.

- **Echo Chambers:** Social media algorithms often create echo chambers by showing users content that aligns with their existing beliefs. Advocates should be aware of this phenomenon and strive to engage with diverse audiences.

- **Online Harassment:** Advocates may face online harassment or backlash in response to their efforts. It is important to have strategies in place for managing and addressing such challenges while maintaining focus on the advocacy goals.

2.6 The Future of Social Media and Advocacy

As social media continues to evolve, its role in advocacy is likely to expand and transform:

- **Integration of Emerging Technologies:** Emerging technologies, such as artificial intelligence and blockchain, may offer new tools for advocacy and activism. These technologies could enhance transparency, security, and engagement in advocacy efforts.

- **Increased Collaboration:** Social media will likely see increased collaboration between organizations, activists, and influencers. By working together, these groups can leverage their collective reach and resources to drive more significant change.

- **Evolving Platforms:** As new social media platforms emerge and existing ones evolve, advocates will need to adapt their strategies to leverage the latest features and trends.

Conclusion

Social media has become a powerful force for advocacy, social change, and community empowerment. By providing a platform for amplifying voices, organizing movements, and engaging with global audiences, social media has transformed how individuals and groups advocate for change. As we continue to navigate the digital landscape, it is essential to recognize and harness the positive potential of social media while addressing the challenges that may arise.

In the next chapter, **Chapter 3: The Economic Impact of Social Media: Transforming Business and Commerce**, we will explore how social media has revolutionized business practices, created new economic opportunities, and reshaped the global marketplace.

Chapter 3: The Economic Impact of Social Media: Transforming Business and Commerce

3.1 Social Media as a Business Tool

Social media has fundamentally transformed the business landscape, providing companies with new ways to connect with customers, market products, and drive sales. Its role extends beyond marketing to influence various aspects of business operations, from customer service to brand management.

Key aspects of social media's impact on business include:

- **Enhanced Customer Engagement:** Social media platforms allow businesses to engage directly with their customers, respond to inquiries, and address concerns in real time. This direct interaction fosters stronger relationships and builds customer loyalty.

- **Targeted Advertising:** Social media advertising offers sophisticated targeting options based on user demographics, interests, and behaviours. This precision allows businesses to reach specific audiences more effectively and optimize their marketing efforts.

- **Brand Building and Awareness:** Social media provides a platform for businesses to build and strengthen their brand identity. Consistent messaging, engaging content, and strategic campaigns help companies increase brand visibility and recognition.

3.2 E-Commerce and Social Media Integration

The integration of e-commerce and social media has created new opportunities for businesses to reach customers and drive sales:

- **Social Commerce:** Social media platforms have incorporated e-commerce features, such as shoppable posts and integrated checkout options. These features allow users to purchase products directly from social media without leaving the platform, streamlining the shopping experience.

- **Influencer Marketing:** Influencer marketing leverages the reach and credibility of social media influencers to promote products and services. By partnering with influencers, businesses can tap into their followers' trust and expand their reach to new audiences.

- **User-Generated Content:** Encouraging customers to share their experiences with products or services on social media can generate authentic, user-generated content. This content serves as valuable social proof and can influence potential buyers.

3.3 Social Media and Market Research

Social media offers valuable insights into market trends, consumer preferences, and competitive dynamics:

- **Customer Feedback:** Social media provides a platform for customers to share their opinions and experiences. Businesses can monitor this feedback to understand customer needs, identify areas for improvement, and make data-driven decisions.

- **Trend Analysis:** Analysing social media conversations and trends helps businesses stay informed about industry developments and consumer interests. This information can guide product development, marketing strategies, and business planning.

- **Competitive Intelligence:** Social media monitoring allows businesses to track competitors' activities, campaigns, and customer interactions. This intelligence helps companies stay competitive and identify opportunities for differentiation and growth.

3.4 The Rise of Small Businesses and Startups

Social media has democratized the business landscape, enabling small businesses and startups to compete with larger corporations:

- **Cost-Effective Marketing:** Social media offers a cost-effective marketing solution for small businesses with limited budgets. By leveraging organic content, targeted ads, and influencer partnerships, small businesses can achieve significant reach and engagement without substantial financial investment.

- **Global Reach:** Social media allows small businesses to reach a global audience, breaking down geographical barriers. This expanded reach opens up new markets and opportunities for growth.

- **Community Building:** Small businesses can use social media to build a loyal community of customers and supporters. Engaging with this community fosters brand loyalty and generates word-of-mouth referrals.

3.5 Social Media Analytics and Performance Measurement

Measuring the effectiveness of social media efforts is crucial for optimizing strategies and achieving business objectives:

- **Key Metrics:** Businesses track key metrics, such as engagement rates, click-through rates, conversion rates, and return on investment (ROI). These metrics provide insights into the performance of social media campaigns and help assess their impact on business goals.

- **Analytics Tools:** Social media analytics tools offer comprehensive data on audience behaviour, content performance, and campaign effectiveness. These tools help businesses make informed decisions and refine their social media strategies.

- **Continuous Improvement:** Regular analysis of social media performance allows businesses to identify successful tactics and areas for improvement. This iterative process ensures that social media efforts remain aligned with business objectives and adapt to changing trends.

3.6 The Future of Social Media in Business

As social media continues to evolve, its role in business is likely to expand and adapt:

- **Integration of Advanced Technologies:** Emerging technologies, such as artificial intelligence and augmented reality, will enhance social media capabilities and offer new opportunities for engagement and personalization.

- **Increased Automation:** Automation tools will become more prevalent, streamlining social media management tasks and enabling businesses to scale their efforts efficiently.

- **Greater Emphasis on Privacy and Data Security:** As privacy concerns grow, businesses will need to prioritize data protection and transparency in their social media practices to build and maintain consumer trust.

Conclusion

Social media has revolutionized the business landscape, offering new tools and opportunities for engagement, marketing, and growth. By leveraging the power of social media, businesses can connect with customers, drive sales, and gain valuable insights into market trends. As social media continues to evolve, businesses must stay informed and adapt their strategies to harness its full potential.

In the next chapter, **Chapter 4: Social Media and the Changing Landscape of Education**, we will explore how social media is transforming education, from enhancing learning experiences to fostering collaboration and professional development.

Chapter 4: Social Media and the Changing Landscape of Education

Social media has profoundly impacted education, reshaping how students learn, educators teach, and professionals develop their careers. It has transformed traditional educational models by providing new opportunities for collaboration, access to resources, and interactive learning. In this chapter, we will explore the various ways social media is revolutionizing education, from enhancing the student experience to facilitating professional development.

4.1 Enhancing Learning Experiences through Social Media

Social media platforms have enhanced learning by making education more interactive, accessible, and engaging. Key benefits include:

- **Access to Educational Resources:** Social media allows students and educators to access a wealth of knowledge, including articles, videos, webinars, and online courses. Platforms like YouTube, LinkedIn Learning, and academic communities on Twitter or Reddit serve as valuable resources for learning and knowledge sharing.

- **Peer-to-Peer Learning:** Social media facilitates peer-to-peer learning by enabling students to connect, collaborate, and exchange knowledge. Online study groups, discussion forums, and collaborative projects encourage students to engage with each other and learn from diverse perspectives.

- **Interactive Learning Environments:** Social media offers an interactive, multimedia-rich learning experience. Platforms such as Instagram and TikTok are increasingly used for educational content creation, where complex topics are broken down into engaging, easily digestible videos and infographics.

- **Real-Time Feedback and Support:** Students can ask questions and receive real-time feedback from teachers, peers, or even experts in various fields through platforms like Twitter and LinkedIn. This immediate access to support enhances the learning process and allows students to clarify doubts quickly.

4.2 Fostering Collaboration and Global Connectivity

Social media has facilitated global collaboration among students, educators, and institutions, breaking down geographical barriers and fostering a more connected learning community.

- **Collaborative Projects:** Tools like Google Docs, Slack, and Microsoft Teams, integrated with social media, allow students to work together on projects from different locations. These platforms encourage teamwork, communication, and the development of critical skills like collaboration and problem-solving.

- **Connecting with Experts and Thought Leaders:** Social media enables students to interact with thought leaders, researchers, and professionals in various fields. Platforms like Twitter and LinkedIn provide opportunities to join discussions, follow influencers, and stay updated on industry trends, making learning more relevant and current.

- **Virtual Classrooms and Online Learning Communities:** Social media supports the creation of virtual classrooms and learning communities where students can participate in courses or join discussions with people from around the world. These platforms have become particularly important with the rise of online education, offering a sense of community even in remote learning environments.

4.3 Professional Development and Lifelong Learning

Social media is an important tool for continuous professional development, helping individuals stay up-to-date with industry advancements, network with peers, and enhance their skills.

- **Networking and Career Opportunities:** Platforms like LinkedIn are specifically designed for professional networking, allowing users to connect with colleagues, mentors, and potential employers. Professionals can use these networks to share their expertise, collaborate with others, and explore job opportunities.

- **Learning New Skills:** Social media platforms offer access to countless tutorials, webinars, and courses across various subjects, making lifelong learning more accessible. Whether it's a coding tutorial on YouTube or a leadership course on LinkedIn Learning, professionals can upskill on their own time.

- **Professional Communities and Knowledge Sharing:** Social media hosts vibrant professional communities where members discuss best practices, share research, and offer advice. For example, educators may join Facebook groups dedicated to teaching strategies, while developers participate in forums like GitHub and Stack Overflow to collaborate on projects.

4.4 The Role of Social Media in Digital Literacy

Digital literacy has become a crucial skill in the 21st century, and social media plays a key role in teaching these competencies. Schools and educators are increasingly integrating social media into their curricula to help students become more digitally literate.

- **Understanding Media and Information Literacy:** As students consume content on platforms like Instagram, TikTok, and Twitter, it is essential that they develop the ability to critically evaluate sources, recognize misinformation, and understand the ethical use of media. Educators are leveraging social media to teach these skills, helping students navigate the digital world responsibly.

- **Building Digital Communication Skills:** Social media also helps students develop strong communication skills, as they learn to express their thoughts clearly and concisely across various platforms. These skills are valuable not only in personal use but also in academic and professional settings.

- **Responsible Social Media Use:** Teaching students to use social media responsibly, from understanding privacy settings to managing their digital footprint, is an essential component of digital literacy education.

4.5 Challenges and Considerations for Social Media in Education

While social media offers numerous benefits, its integration into education presents challenges and considerations that must be addressed.

- **Misinformation and Content Credibility:** One of the challenges in using social media for educational purposes is the prevalence of misinformation. Educators must teach students how to verify sources and critically assess the credibility of information they encounter online.

- **Distraction and Overuse:** Social media can also be a source of distraction for students, especially if not managed appropriately. Schools and educators need to establish guidelines for appropriate use and help students balance their social media engagement with their academic responsibilities.

- **Privacy and Data Security:** Protecting students' privacy and data security is critical when using social media for educational purposes. Educators must be mindful of the platforms they use and ensure that students' personal information is safeguarded.

4.6 The Future of Social Media in Education

The role of social media in education is likely to expand and evolve, with emerging technologies and new platforms further transforming the educational landscape.

- **Integration of Virtual and Augmented Reality:** Virtual and augmented reality tools are being integrated with social media to create immersive learning experiences. These technologies offer new ways to visualize complex concepts, conduct virtual field trips, and engage with interactive simulations.

- **Personalized Learning Experiences:** Artificial intelligence and data analytics are being used to create personalized learning experiences on social media platforms. These technologies can tailor content based on individual learning styles and preferences, enhancing student engagement and success.

- **Gamification of Learning:** The gamification of educational content, using game-like elements such as challenges, leaderboards, and rewards, is becoming more prevalent on social media platforms. Gamification can make learning more engaging and motivate students to achieve their educational goals.

Conclusion

Social media has undeniably transformed education, offering new avenues for learning, collaboration, and professional development. From making educational content more accessible to fostering global connectivity and peer learning, social media continues to reshape how students and professionals approach learning. As educators and institutions continue to embrace these tools, it is essential to strike a balance between maximizing their potential and addressing the challenges they present.

In the next chapter, **Chapter 5: Building Communities and Strengthening Connections**, we will explore how social media fosters community building, facilitates cultural exchange, and strengthens social bonds in our increasingly digital world.

Chapter 5: Building Communities and Strengthening Connections

Social media has redefined how people form communities, connect with one another, and share cultural experiences. It serves as a powerful tool for building relationships, fostering cultural exchange, and creating a sense of belonging in an increasingly globalized world. In this chapter, we will explore how social media helps strengthen social bonds, facilitates cultural understanding, and supports the development of both local and global communities.

5.1 The Rise of Digital Communities

One of the most significant impacts of social media is its ability to create and nurture digital communities. Unlike traditional physical communities, these virtual groups transcend geographical boundaries and bring together individuals with shared interests, beliefs, or experiences.

- **Interest-Based Communities:** Platforms like Reddit, Facebook Groups, and specialized forums allow people to connect with others who share their passions - whether it's gaming, gardening, technology, or wellness. These interest-based communities enable users to exchange ideas, share resources, and support one another in personal growth or hobbies.

- **Support Networks:** Social media plays an essential role in providing support networks for individuals dealing with personal challenges, such as mental health issues, chronic illnesses, or parenting. These online support groups allow users to share their stories, receive advice, and find comfort from those facing similar struggles.

- **Local and Neighbourhood Groups:** Social media has also transformed how local communities organize and communicate. Neighbourhood groups on platforms like Facebook and Nextdoor enable residents to share updates, discuss local issues, organize events, and offer mutual aid, fostering a stronger sense of community in real life.

5.2 Social Media and Cultural Exchange

Social media platforms have become global hubs for cultural exchange, where individuals can share their unique traditions, languages, and perspectives with people from different parts of the world. This exchange promotes greater understanding, tolerance, and appreciation of cultural diversity.

- **Celebrating Diversity:** Instagram, TikTok, and YouTube are full of creators who use their platforms to showcase their cultures, traditions, and identities. These creators help bridge cultural gaps by exposing others to new food, fashion, art, and customs, fostering global awareness and acceptance.

- **Language Learning and Cultural Immersion:** Social media has given rise to informal language learning communities, where users help one another practice new languages. Apps like HelloTalk and groups on platforms such as Reddit or Discord connect language learners with native speakers, encouraging cross-cultural dialogue and understanding.

- **Global Collaboration in Art and Music:** Social media allows artists and musicians to collaborate across borders, blending different cultural influences and creating new, hybrid forms of expression. Platforms like

SoundCloud, DeviantArt, and TikTok facilitate creative exchange, leading to cultural fusion in art, music, and other forms of expression.

5.3 Strengthening Family and Personal Connections

Beyond building new communities, social media has strengthened existing personal connections by providing an easy way to stay in touch with friends, family, and loved ones, no matter the distance.

- **Keeping Families Connected:** Social media platforms such as Facebook, WhatsApp, and Instagram make it easier for families to stay connected, especially when living far apart. Through video calls, group chats, and photo-sharing, families can maintain close ties despite physical distance.

- **Reconnecting with Old Friends:** Platforms like Facebook have made it possible for individuals to reconnect with long-lost friends or former classmates. These platforms provide opportunities to rekindle relationships that might have otherwise been lost.

- **Strengthening Romantic Relationships:** Social media has facilitated long-distance romantic relationships by providing couples with tools for daily communication. From sharing moments via Instagram Stories to video calls on Messenger or WhatsApp, social media helps couples feel more connected.

5.4 Social Media as a Tool for Social Inclusion

Social media has played an important role in promoting social inclusion by providing a platform for underrepresented or marginalized groups to connect, share their experiences, and advocate for their rights.

- **LGBTQ+ Communities:** Social media offers safe spaces for LGBTQ+ individuals to connect, share stories, and find support. Platforms like Twitter, Tumblr, and TikTok have vibrant LGBTQ+ communities that provide a sense of belonging and validation for individuals who may face discrimination or isolation in their offline lives.

- **Disability Advocacy and Support:** Online communities for people with disabilities offer spaces where users can discuss accessibility issues, share resources, and support one another. These communities also serve as platforms for advocacy, raising awareness about disability rights and pushing for greater inclusivity in society.

- **Ethnic and Religious Communities:** Social media allows ethnic and religious groups to connect, celebrate their identities, and find solidarity. These online spaces enable users to engage with cultural practices, share religious teachings, and organize community events, even when physical gatherings may not be possible.

5.5 Challenges in Community Building on Social Media

While social media has created immense opportunities for community building and connection, it also presents several challenges that can impact the quality and sustainability of these digital relationships.

- **Echo Chambers and Polarization:** Social media algorithms often show users content that aligns with their existing views, leading to the formation of echo chambers where dissenting opinions are rarely encountered. This can contribute to social polarization and reinforce divisions within communities.

- **Online Harassment and Trolling:** Digital communities can sometimes be disrupted by online harassment, trolling, and cyberbullying. For some users, these negative experiences may discourage participation in online spaces and undermine the sense of safety and belonging.

- **Superficial Connections:** While social media allows for broad connectivity, the quality of these relationships can sometimes be shallow or fleeting. Some critics argue that online interactions lack the depth and emotional richness of face-to-face communication, leading to feelings of loneliness or disconnection.

5.6 The Future of Online Communities

As social media platforms evolve, so too will the ways in which people form and maintain communities. The future of online communities will likely be shaped by emerging technologies, shifting cultural norms, and increasing awareness of social media's impact on society.

- **Integration of Virtual and Augmented Reality:** The rise of virtual and augmented reality (VR and AR) platforms will transform digital communities by creating immersive environments where users can interact in more lifelike and engaging ways. Platforms like Meta's Horizon Worlds and VRChat are early examples of this shift, offering users the opportunity to form deeper, more personal connections.

- **Decentralized Social Networks:** Blockchain technology is paving the way for decentralized social networks, where users have greater control over their data and interactions. These platforms, like Mastodon or Minds, allow for more autonomy and privacy in community building while promoting user-driven content moderation.

- **Fostering Empathy and Inclusion:** As the world becomes increasingly connected, there is growing awareness of the need to foster empathy and inclusion in digital spaces. Social media platforms may implement features that encourage more meaningful interactions and reduce the impact of toxic behaviours, helping to create more inclusive and supportive online communities.

Conclusion

Social media has transformed the way we build communities, form connections, and engage in cultural exchange. By fostering interest-based groups, supporting underrepresented voices, and strengthening personal relationships, social media has become a vital tool for community building in the modern world. However, it also poses challenges, including the risks of polarization, online harassment, and shallow connections. As new technologies emerge and platforms evolve, the future of online communities will continue to adapt, offering new opportunities for deeper and more meaningful engagement.

In the next chapter, **Chapter 6: Social Media and Mental Health: A Double-Edged Sword**, we will examine the complex relationship between social media and mental well-being, exploring both the positive and negative effects of social media use on mental health.

Chapter 6: Social Media and Mental Health: A Double-Edged Sword

Social media has become deeply ingrained in modern life, affecting how we communicate, interact, and view ourselves. While it offers many benefits, such as connectivity and access to information, it also has significant implications for mental health. In this chapter, we explore the complex relationship between social media and mental well-being, examining both the positive and negative effects of its use.

6.1 The Positive Effects of Social Media on Mental Health

While much attention is given to the harmful effects of social media, it's important to recognize its potential to positively impact mental well-being. Several aspects of social media use can enhance individuals' mental health, providing emotional support, fostering community, and enabling self-expression.

- **Emotional Support and Connection:** For many, social media offers a platform for emotional support, allowing users to connect with friends, family, or support groups when facing personal challenges. Platforms like Facebook, Instagram, and Twitter allow users to share their feelings, receive encouragement, and feel connected, which can reduce feelings of isolation or loneliness.

- **Access to Mental Health Resources:** Social media provides access to mental health information, resources, and support services. Organizations, influencers, and mental health professionals use platforms like YouTube, Instagram, and TikTok to share tips, strategies, and information on coping with stress, anxiety, depression, and other mental health issues. These resources can make mental health care more accessible to a global audience.

- **Fostering Self-Expression and Creativity:** Platforms like Instagram, YouTube, and TikTok allow users to express themselves creatively, whether through art, music, writing, or video content. For many, this form of self-expression can be therapeutic, providing an outlet for emotions and personal experiences. This can promote self-esteem and self-awareness, contributing to better mental health.

- **Support for Marginalized Groups:** Social media can be a lifeline for individuals from marginalized communities, including LGBTQ+ people, people of colour, or those living with disabilities. Online communities offer a safe space to share experiences, find support, and feel validated, helping to reduce feelings of alienation and discrimination.

6.2 The Negative Impact of Social Media on Mental Health

Despite its potential benefits, social media can also have detrimental effects on mental health. The way social media platforms are designed - often prioritizing engagement and attention - can contribute to various psychological issues.

- **Social Comparison and Low Self-Esteem:** Social media encourages users to compare themselves to others, whether it's their appearance, achievements, or lifestyle. Constant exposure to curated, idealized images of others' lives can lead to feelings of inadequacy, low self-esteem, and even depression. Instagram, for example, is often cited as a platform where users, particularly young women, experience negative body image due to unrealistic beauty standards.

- **Fear of Missing Out (FOMO):** The fear of missing out, or FOMO, is a psychological phenomenon exacerbated by social media. As users see their friends and acquaintances attending events, traveling, or achieving milestones, they may feel left out or inadequate. This sense of exclusion can lead to anxiety, stress, and dissatisfaction with one's own life.

- **Addictive Behaviour:** Many social media platforms are designed to keep users engaged for as long as possible, often leading to compulsive checking of notifications and continuous scrolling. This can create addictive behaviour, where users struggle to disconnect, affecting their productivity, relationships, and mental well-being.

- **Cyberbullying and Online Harassment:** Social media has given rise to cyberbullying, where individuals are harassed, threatened, or humiliated online. Platforms like Twitter, Instagram, and TikTok can be breeding grounds for trolling, harassment, and bullying, particularly among younger users. The emotional toll of cyberbullying can lead to anxiety, depression, and even suicidal thoughts.

- **Sleep Disruption:** Excessive social media use, particularly at night, can disrupt sleep patterns and negatively impact mental health. The blue light emitted by screens, combined with the stimulation of social media, can interfere with the body's natural sleep cycle, leading to insomnia and increased feelings of stress or fatigue.

6.3 Understanding the Balance: How Much Is Too Much?

Finding a balance between healthy social media use and its potential negative effects is crucial for mental well-being. The key is to develop mindful habits that allow individuals to enjoy the benefits of social media while mitigating its risks.

- **Setting Boundaries:** Setting limits on the time spent on social media can help reduce its negative impact on mental health. Features like "screen time" trackers on smartphones or app-specific usage limits can be helpful tools in managing social media consumption.

- **Curating Content and Connections:** Social media users have the power to curate their feeds by following accounts that inspire positivity and unfollowing those that trigger stress, anxiety, or self-doubt. Surrounding oneself with supportive, uplifting content can help combat negative emotions.

- **Practicing Digital Detox:** Taking breaks from social media, whether for a few hours, days, or even weeks, can be beneficial for mental health. A digital detox allows individuals to disconnect from the pressures of online interaction and focus on real-world connections and experiences.

6.4 The Role of Social Media Platforms in Mental Health

As awareness of the impact of social media on mental health grows, platforms are beginning to take steps to mitigate harm and promote positive well-being. While the responsibility also lies with users, platforms play a significant role in shaping the digital environment.

- **Wellness Tools and Features:** Platforms like Instagram, Facebook, and TikTok have introduced tools to promote digital wellness, such as screen time reminders, notification controls, and "Take a Break" prompts. These features are designed to encourage users to reflect on their social media habits and take steps to protect their mental well-being.

- **Tackling Cyberbullying and Harassment:** Many social media platforms have implemented stricter policies and tools to combat cyberbullying and online harassment. These include reporting mechanisms, content moderation, and the ability to block or mute harmful accounts. However, these efforts are ongoing and continue to evolve as platforms respond to new challenges.

- **Mental Health Campaigns:** Some platforms actively participate in mental health awareness campaigns, collaborating with mental health organizations to promote resources and support. For example, Instagram has partnered with mental health charities to offer resources and helplines directly through the app when users search for certain terms related to mental health crises.

6.5 Strategies for Healthy Social Media Use

To maximize the positive impact of social media on mental health while minimizing its negative effects, users can adopt various strategies for mindful engagement.

- **Mindful Consumption:** Instead of passively scrolling through social media, individuals can engage mindfully by being intentional about the content they consume. Asking questions like, "How does this content make me feel?" can help users make conscious decisions about what they view and who they follow.

- **Fostering Meaningful Interactions:** Rather than focusing on accumulating likes, followers, or comments, users should prioritize meaningful interactions with others. Engaging in genuine conversations, offering support, and building real connections can enhance the social aspect of social media and contribute to positive mental health.

- **Maintaining a Balanced Lifestyle:** It's essential to balance online engagement with offline activities. Physical exercise, outdoor activities, face-to-face interactions, and hobbies provide essential breaks from the digital world and contribute to mental well-being.

6.6 The Future of Social Media and Mental Health

The intersection of social media and mental health will continue to evolve as platforms, users, and policymakers explore ways to create healthier online environments. Emerging technologies, shifting cultural norms, and increased awareness will shape the future of this relationship.

- **Artificial Intelligence and Mental Health Monitoring:** In the future, artificial intelligence (AI) could play a more prominent role in monitoring user behaviour for signs of mental distress. Social media platforms may implement AI tools that offer support to users experiencing emotional difficulties, such as identifying concerning posts and directing them to mental health resources.

- **Promoting Digital Well-Being:** As mental health awareness grows, social media platforms may prioritize features that promote digital well-being. New tools and settings could help users better manage their time, reduce exposure to harmful content, and foster more meaningful interactions online.

- **Cultural Shifts in Social Media Use:** As individuals become more aware of the impact of social media on mental health, cultural norms around its use may shift. Instead of focusing on social validation and status, there may be a growing emphasis on authenticity, self-care, and well-being in online interactions.

Conclusion

Social media is a double-edged sword when it comes to mental health. On one hand, it offers opportunities for emotional support, self-expression, and community building. On the other, it poses risks like social comparison, cyberbullying, and addiction. Navigating the complexities of social media requires mindfulness, balance, and a conscious effort to engage in positive, meaningful interactions. As platforms evolve and awareness of mental health grows, there is hope that social media can continue to be a force for good in promoting well-being.

In the next chapter, **Chapter 7: Social Media and Political Engagement: Strengthening Democracy or Sowing Division?**, we will explore the role social media plays in political discourse, its impact on democracy, and the challenges it presents in maintaining informed and civil political engagement.

Chapter 7: Social Media and Political Engagement: Strengthening Democracy or Sowing Division?

Social media has transformed political engagement, altering the way citizens

participate in democratic processes, access information, and express their views.

While it offers unprecedented opportunities for political involvement, social media

also presents significant challenges that can undermine democratic ideals. This

chapter explores the dual role of social media in strengthening democracy and

contributing to political polarization, misinformation, and division.

7.1 The Positive Impact of Social Media on Political Engagement

Social media has become a powerful tool for political engagement, providing a

platform for greater participation, transparency, and direct communication between

citizens and their leaders. Several key benefits demonstrate its potential to

strengthen democratic processes:

- **Increased Access to Information:** Social media allows users to access real-
  time updates on political developments, news, and policy debates. Platforms
  such as Twitter and Facebook serve as valuable resources for disseminating
  information, giving citizens greater access to political knowledge, including
  from alternative or independent sources not covered by traditional media.

- **Direct Communication with Leaders:** Social media provides a direct line
  of communication between citizens and political leaders. Politicians use
  platforms like Twitter and Facebook to share their viewpoints, explain

policies, and engage directly with constituents. This two-way interaction fosters greater transparency and accountability in governance.

- **Empowering Grassroots Movements:** Social media has lowered barriers to political organization, allowing grassroots movements to form, grow, and mobilize supporters quickly. From local initiatives to global movements, platforms enable groups to rally behind a cause, organize protests, and petition for change with minimal financial or logistical hurdles.

- **Encouraging Civic Participation:** Social media can inspire civic engagement by facilitating voter registration drives, political discussion forums, and campaigns promoting participation in elections. By making political information more accessible and engaging, platforms contribute to an informed and active electorate.

7.2 How Social Media Has Changed Political Campaigns

Social media has dramatically reshaped how political campaigns are conducted, providing new ways to communicate with voters and influence public opinion.

- **Targeted Campaigning:** Social media platforms enable highly targeted political advertising based on user data, allowing campaigns to tailor messages to specific demographics, interests, or geographic locations. This micro-targeting allows candidates to speak directly to particular voter groups, maximizing the effectiveness of their campaigns.

- **Viral Political Messaging:** Social media offers the potential for political messages to go viral, rapidly reaching millions of people. Short videos, memes, or tweets with powerful messages can quickly spread across platforms, amplifying political campaigns and mobilizing supporters.

- **User-Generated Content:** Campaigns can harness the power of user-generated content, encouraging supporters to share messages, create memes, and spread the word. This grassroots-style promotion can build momentum and create a sense of collective effort.

- **Real-Time Response:** Social media allows candidates and political parties to respond instantly to developments, critiques, or attacks. Politicians can issue statements, clarify their positions, and counter misinformation in real-time, helping to manage their public image and control the narrative.

7.3 The Role of Social Media in Fostering Political Polarization

While social media can enhance political engagement, it has also been criticized for contributing to political polarization and division. Several dynamics within social media ecosystems foster these divides:

- **Echo Chambers and Filter Bubbles:** Social media algorithms are designed to prioritize content that aligns with users' existing views and interests. This creates echo chambers, where users are primarily exposed to information that reinforces their beliefs. Filter bubbles reduce the diversity of viewpoints users encounter, making it harder to engage with differing perspectives and fostering polarization.

- **Amplification of Extreme Views:** Social media platforms often prioritize content that generates strong emotional reactions - such as outrage, anger, or fear -because it drives more engagement. As a result, extreme political views or inflammatory content can gain more visibility, contributing to political radicalization and divisive discourse.

- **Disinformation and Fake News:** The rapid spread of misinformation and disinformation on social media can distort public understanding of political issues. False narratives, conspiracy theories, and manipulated content can spread quickly, leading to confusion and deepening political divides. This erosion of trust in credible sources of information has serious implications for democracy.

7.4 The Role of Social Media in Political Movements

Social media has played a central role in organizing and amplifying political movements around the world. By giving ordinary people a platform to voice their concerns and unite around causes, social media has facilitated significant political and social change.

- **Arab Spring:** Social media was instrumental during the Arab Spring uprisings, where platforms like Facebook and Twitter were used to organize protests, share information, and mobilize the public. Activists used these tools to challenge authoritarian regimes, communicate with global audiences, and advocate for democratic reforms.

- **Hong Kong Protests:** During the pro-democracy protests in Hong Kong, social media was used to organize demonstrations, coordinate actions, and share information about police movements. Activists also used platforms to bring global attention to their cause, seeking solidarity from international supporters.

- **Occupy Wall Street:** Social media played a key role in the Occupy Wall Street movement, where protesters used platforms like Twitter and Facebook to organize events, share experiences, and challenge economic inequality. The movement's slogan, "We are the 99%," spread rapidly through social media, galvanizing support and drawing attention to wealth disparities.

7.5 The Challenges of Social Media in Maintaining Civil Political Discourse

While social media has democratized political discourse, it also presents challenges in maintaining civility, accuracy, and productive debate in political discussions.

- **Anonymity and Toxicity:** The anonymity provided by social media can encourage uncivil behaviour, with users engaging in name-calling, insults, or harassment. Political discussions can quickly become hostile, reducing the possibility of constructive dialogue and deepening divisions.

- **The Rise of "Fake News" and Conspiracy Theories:** Social media platforms have been criticized for their role in the proliferation of "fake news" and conspiracy theories, which can skew political discourse and undermine trust in democratic institutions. The spread of false information on platforms like Facebook and Twitter often goes unchecked, contributing to political misinformation and eroding informed debate.

- **Manipulation and Influence Operations:** Foreign and domestic actors have used social media to manipulate political discourse, influence elections, and sow division. Notable examples include Russian interference in the 2016 U.S. presidential election, where disinformation campaigns were launched to inflame political tensions and shape public opinion.

7.6 Social Media as a Tool for Civic Education and Political Literacy

Despite its challenges, social media can also be a valuable tool for promoting civic education and political literacy. By encouraging informed participation and discourse, platforms have the potential to contribute to a more educated electorate.

- **Promoting Informed Voting:** Social media can be used to share accurate, non-partisan information about candidates, policies, and election processes. By providing access to voter guides, policy comparisons, and fact-checked news, social media can help voters make informed decisions.

- **Political Debate and Public Forums:** Platforms like Twitter, Reddit, and Facebook can serve as public forums for political debate, allowing users to discuss policies, question candidates, and share perspectives. These discussions can foster critical thinking and encourage citizens to engage with political issues more deeply.

- **Encouraging Youth Participation:** Social media has proven particularly effective in engaging younger generations in politics. By using platforms familiar to young people, campaigns and movements can inspire political activism and participation among a demographic that is often less engaged in traditional political processes.

7.7 The Future of Social Media and Political Engagement

As social media continues to evolve, so too will its role in political engagement. Emerging technologies, changing regulations, and shifting cultural norms will shape the future of political discourse online.

- **Regulation and Content Moderation:** Governments and social media platforms are increasingly focused on addressing issues like misinformation, hate speech, and manipulation. Future regulations may impose stricter content moderation policies, transparency in political advertising, and measures to protect electoral integrity.

- **The Rise of New Platforms:** As social media landscapes shift, new platforms may emerge as the dominant forces in political discourse. Platforms like TikTok, with its younger demographic, are already shaping political engagement in unique ways. Future platforms may prioritize different formats, features, and community standards, further altering the nature of political participation.

- **AI and Political Messaging:** Advances in artificial intelligence (AI) could change how political campaigns are run, with AI tools helping candidates tailor messages, identify voter concerns, and optimize engagement strategies. However, AI could also be used to spread disinformation or manipulate public opinion, raising ethical concerns.

Conclusion

Social media has fundamentally transformed political engagement, offering new ways to participate, access information, and hold leaders accountable. However, it has also introduced significant challenges, including political polarization, the spread of misinformation, and uncivil discourse. As we move forward, it is essential to strike a balance between harnessing the potential of social media to strengthen democracy while addressing the risks it presents.

In the next chapter, **Chapter 8: The Role of Social Media in Business Innovation and Entrepreneurship**, we will explore how social media is driving innovation in business, creating new opportunities for entrepreneurs, and reshaping traditional industries.

Chapter 8: The Role of Social Media in Business Innovation and Entrepreneurship

Social media has not only transformed personal communication and political

engagement but has also revolutionized the business landscape. It serves as a powerful tool for innovation, entrepreneurship, and the reimagining of traditional industries. From marketing and customer engagement to creating entirely new business models, social media has reshaped the way businesses operate and grow in the digital age.

8.1 Social Media as a Catalyst for Business Innovation

Social media platforms have become integral to business strategies, providing companies with the ability to reach vast audiences, engage with consumers in real-time, and drive innovation. Several key areas highlight how social media serves as a catalyst for innovation:

- **Real-Time Market Research and Feedback:** Businesses can use social media to gather insights directly from their audience. Through polls, comments, and social listening tools, companies can learn what their customers want and quickly adapt products, services, or campaigns. This constant feedback loop enables businesses to innovate faster, responding to changing consumer needs and preferences.

- **Crowdsourcing Ideas:** Social media allows businesses to involve their customers in the innovation process through crowdsourcing. Whether it's asking followers for product ideas or feedback on new features, platforms like Instagram, Twitter, and LinkedIn provide businesses with a direct line to their audience's creativity and preferences. This collaborative innovation approach helps in product development and problem-solving.

- **Brand Storytelling and Personalization:** The rise of social media has encouraged brands to innovate in how they connect with consumers. Businesses are increasingly focused on storytelling, using platforms to share their brand's history, values, and mission in a more personal and engaging way. Personalization of content, which social media facilitates through data and user interaction, allows businesses to create customized experiences, further building consumer loyalty and engagement.

- **Data-Driven Decision Making:** Social media platforms provide a treasure trove of data that businesses can analyse to optimize their strategies. Insights from social media analytics can inform decisions on customer preferences, emerging trends, campaign effectiveness, and more. This ability to make data-driven decisions in real-time enhances business agility and fosters innovation.

8.2 Social Media as an Entrepreneurial Launchpad

Social media has played a significant role in lowering the barriers to entry for aspiring entrepreneurs, allowing them to reach global audiences, build brands, and scale businesses with minimal overhead costs.

- **Cost-Effective Marketing:** Platforms like Instagram, Facebook, TikTok, and LinkedIn provide entrepreneurs with access to millions of users without the high costs associated with traditional advertising. Organic reach, paid ads, and influencer partnerships enable small businesses and startups to build brand visibility quickly and efficiently.

- **E-Commerce Integration:** Social media platforms have integrated e-commerce functionalities, making it easier than ever for entrepreneurs to sell directly to consumers. Platforms like Instagram and Facebook allow businesses to create online shops, facilitating seamless shopping experiences within the app. This integration has opened up new revenue streams for businesses of all sizes, enabling entrepreneurs to launch and grow their e-commerce ventures with little to no initial investment.

- **Influencer Marketing:** Entrepreneurs are leveraging the power of influencer marketing to drive brand awareness and sales. By partnering with influencers who align with their brand values and target audience, small businesses can tap into large, engaged followings without spending vast sums on traditional advertising. Influencers often serve as brand advocates, helping startups gain credibility and trust among potential customers.

- **Building and Engaging Communities:** Entrepreneurs use social media to build loyal communities around their products or services. Platforms like Facebook Groups, Discord, and Reddit enable businesses to engage directly with their customers, providing support, gathering feedback, and fostering brand loyalty. This sense of community can lead to organic growth as satisfied customers share their experiences with others.

8.3 The Rise of Social Commerce

Social media has given birth to "social commerce," a fusion of social media and online shopping. This emerging trend allows businesses to reach consumers where they spend much of their time - on social platforms - while reducing friction in the purchasing process.

- **Shoppable Posts and Ads:** Social media platforms like Instagram and Pinterest offer shoppable posts and ads, allowing users to buy products directly from the app. This seamless integration of content and commerce has revolutionized the shopping experience, making it easier for businesses to convert engagement into sales.

- **Live Shopping Events:** Live shopping is gaining traction as a popular social commerce trend. Platforms like Instagram Live, Facebook Live, and TikTok allow businesses to showcase products in real-time, interact with viewers, and encourage immediate purchases. This live engagement adds an interactive element to online shopping, making it more personal and immersive.

- **Peer-to-Peer Sales and Recommendations:** Social media has also boosted peer-to-peer sales, where users recommend products to friends and followers. Platforms like Pinterest and Facebook Marketplace enable users to sell items directly to others, while Instagram influencers and YouTube creators promote products based on personal experiences. This peer-driven commerce model creates a more authentic and trustworthy shopping environment.

8.4 Traditional Industries Disrupted by Social Media

Social media has been a disruptive force across several industries, compelling traditional businesses to adapt to new digital realities. Some of the most affected sectors include:

- **Retail and Fashion:** Social media has fundamentally changed the way consumers shop for fashion and lifestyle products. Brands now rely on social media influencers and user-generated content to create buzz around new collections. Fast fashion companies, in particular, use platforms like Instagram and TikTok to promote their products and engage with younger consumers who favour digital shopping experiences.

- **Entertainment and Media:** The entertainment industry has also been transformed by social media, which offers new ways to consume content. YouTube, TikTok, and Instagram have given rise to a new generation of creators, allowing individuals to build large audiences without the backing of traditional media companies. Social media has also disrupted film and television marketing, with trailers, interviews, and behind-the-scenes content now primarily promoted through platforms like Twitter and Instagram.

- **Hospitality and Travel:** In the hospitality and travel industry, social media is a key tool for customer engagement and brand loyalty. Hotels, airlines, and travel agencies use platforms like Instagram and TripAdvisor to showcase destinations, offer promotions, and respond to customer inquiries. User-generated content, such as travel photos and reviews, has become an essential part of the marketing strategy in this sector.

- **Food and Beverage:** The rise of "foodstagramming" and social media influencers in the food space has reshaped how restaurants and food brands market themselves. Platforms like Instagram and TikTok are key drivers of food trends, allowing new restaurants, food trucks, and products to gain popularity rapidly. Viral challenges, recipe videos, and visually appealing dishes posted by users have all contributed to this shift in marketing.

8.5 Success Stories: Entrepreneurs Who Built Businesses on Social Media

Many successful entrepreneurs have leveraged the power of social media to launch and grow their businesses, building brands that thrive in the digital age. Some notable examples include:

- **Kylie Jenner (Kylie Cosmetics):** Kylie Jenner used her vast Instagram following to build a multi-million-dollar beauty empire, Kylie Cosmetics. By leveraging her personal brand and directly engaging with followers, she was able to promote her products and grow her company without relying on traditional advertising or retail partnerships.

- **Glossier:** Emily Weiss, founder of the beauty brand Glossier, started her company after building a successful beauty blog and engaging directly with her social media followers. Glossier's "Instagram-first" marketing strategy helped the brand create a loyal community, leading to its rapid growth and success in the beauty industry.

- **Gymshark:** Gymshark, a fitness apparel company founded by Ben Francis, grew its business largely through influencer partnerships and a strong presence on platforms like Instagram and YouTube. By connecting with fitness influencers and sharing user-generated content, Gymshark built a brand with a cult-like following and became a major player in the fitness industry.

8.6 Challenges of Building a Business on Social Media

While social media provides opportunities for entrepreneurs, it also presents several challenges:

- **Platform Dependency:** Businesses that rely too heavily on a single social media platform may face risks if the platform changes its algorithms, policies, or monetization strategies. Diversifying across multiple platforms is essential to mitigate this risk.

- **Managing Public Perception:** Social media's openness makes it easy for businesses to interact with customers, but it also exposes them to criticism and backlash. Managing online reputation and responding to negative feedback quickly and effectively is crucial for maintaining a positive public image.

- **Content Saturation:** As more businesses use social media to market their products and services, competition for attention has intensified. Standing out in a crowded digital space requires creativity, consistent engagement, and a deep understanding of what resonates with the target audience.

8.7 The Future of Social Media in Business and Entrepreneurship

As social media continues to evolve, so too will its role in business innovation and entrepreneurship:

- **AI and Automation:** Artificial intelligence and automation will play an increasingly significant role in social media marketing. Chatbots, AI-powered content creation, and personalized ad targeting will allow businesses to interact with customers more efficiently and deliver highly tailored experiences.

- **Augmented Reality (AR) Shopping:** Social media platforms are beginning to integrate augmented reality (AR) into their shopping features. This technology will allow customers to virtually try on products, such as clothing, accessories, or makeup, directly through social media apps, further blending the line between content and commerce.

- **Blockchain and Decentralized Social Media:** Blockchain technology could enable decentralized social media platforms, offering new opportunities for entrepreneurs and businesses to engage with consumers in more secure, transparent, and trust-based ecosystems. This shift could also provide more control over content monetization and data privacy.

Conclusion

Social media has profoundly impacted business innovation and entrepreneurship, offering new tools, opportunities, and strategies for growth in the digital age. From fostering direct engagement with consumers to creating entirely new commerce models, social media has become an indispensable part of modern business. However, as the landscape continues to evolve, businesses must adapt to new challenges, trends, and technologies to remain competitive.

In the next chapter, **Chapter 9: Social Media and Data Privacy: Balancing Innovation with Security**, we will explore the complex relationship between social media platforms and data privacy, focusing on the challenges of balancing

innovation with the need to protect user information.

Chapter 9: Social Media and Data Privacy: Balancing Innovation with Security

In an age where social media platforms have become a central part of daily life, the

issue of data privacy has emerged as one of the most pressing concerns. The vast

amount of personal information shared on social media platforms provides

opportunities for innovation, targeted services, and personalized experiences, but it

also exposes users to risks. This chapter explores the complex relationship between

social media platforms and data privacy, delving into the challenges of balancing

innovation with the need to protect user information.

9.1 The Data Economy: How Social Media Platforms Utilize User Data

Social media platforms operate in a data-driven economy, where user information is

the cornerstone of their business models. Every interaction - whether it's a like, a

comment, a share, or even time spent on a post - generates data. This data is

leveraged to enhance user experiences and drive innovation, but it also fuels the

advertising engine that powers these platforms.

- **Personalization and Targeted Advertising:** One of the most common uses
  of user data is personalization. Platforms use algorithms to analyse user

behaviour and preferences, delivering content that is tailored to individual tastes. This personalization extends to targeted advertising, where ads are shown based on a user's online activity, interests, and demographic information. While this creates more relevant experiences for users, it raises concerns about the extent to which personal data is being collected and analysed.

- **Data Monetization:** Social media platforms offer free access to users, but in exchange, they monetize user data through advertising. This business model has sparked debates about the ethical implications of data collection. While users may benefit from free services, their personal information is often sold to third-party advertisers or used to develop advanced marketing strategies.

- **Innovative Services:** Data collected from users is also used to create innovative services such as predictive analytics, recommendation systems, and AI-driven content creation. By understanding user behaviour, platforms can suggest friends, curate content, and recommend products, enhancing the overall social media experience. However, this innovation comes with a cost—the more data collected, the more exposed users become to potential privacy violations.

9.2 Privacy Concerns: The Risks of Data Collection

As social media platforms collect more data, concerns about privacy risks have grown. While these platforms provide immense value through personalized experiences and innovations, they also expose users to a range of vulnerabilities:

- **Data Breaches and Hacks:** Social media platforms are prime targets for cyberattacks, given the vast amounts of personal data they store. Data breaches can lead to the exposure of sensitive information such as email addresses, passwords, and even private messages. High-profile breaches, like the Facebook-Cambridge Analytica scandal, have raised awareness about the potential misuse of personal data.

- **Third-Party Data Sharing:** Many social media platforms share user data with third-party applications and advertisers. While this may enhance the functionality of services or improve ad targeting, it raises questions about how much control users have over their data once it leaves the platform. Often, users are unaware of the extent to which their data is being shared with external entities.

- **Surveillance and Profiling:** The data collected on social media can be used for surveillance and profiling, both by governments and private organizations. In some cases, governments may monitor social media for political dissent or criminal activity, which can infringe on personal freedoms. Additionally, advertisers use data to create detailed profiles of individuals, which can be used to influence purchasing decisions or even political opinions.

9.3 The Legal and Regulatory Landscape

In response to growing concerns over data privacy, governments around the world have begun to implement stricter regulations to protect user data. These regulations aim to strike a balance between enabling innovation and ensuring that personal information is protected.

- **The General Data Protection Regulation (GDPR):** Enforced in 2018, the GDPR is a comprehensive data protection law in the European Union that sets strict guidelines on how businesses collect, store, and use personal data. Under the GDPR, users have the right to know what data is being collected, request the deletion of their data, and withdraw consent for data processing. The regulation has significantly impacted social media platforms, forcing them to rethink their data collection and sharing practices.

- **California Consumer Privacy Act (CCPA):** The CCPA is one of the most comprehensive privacy laws in the United States. Similar to the GDPR, it gives users greater control over their personal data, including the right to access, delete, and opt-out of the sale of their data. Social media platforms operating in California must comply with these regulations, further highlighting the global push for stronger privacy protections.

- **Evolving Global Standards:** Beyond the GDPR and CCPA, other countries are beginning to implement or strengthen their privacy laws. In many regions, there is growing recognition that protecting personal data is essential for maintaining user trust in digital platforms. These regulations are likely to become more stringent as data collection practices become more sophisticated.

9.4 Balancing Innovation with Privacy

The challenge for social media platforms lies in finding the right balance between fostering innovation and protecting user privacy. While the collection of data is necessary for improving services, it must be done responsibly and transparently.

- **Transparency and User Consent:** One of the key principles of data privacy is transparency. Social media platforms must clearly communicate to users what data is being collected, how it is used, and with whom it is shared. Consent should be obtained in an informed manner, giving users the option to control their data. Platforms like Facebook, Twitter, and Instagram have already taken steps to improve transparency by providing users with detailed privacy settings and options to manage their data.

- **Data Minimization:** Another important approach to balancing innovation with privacy is data minimization. This involves collecting only the data that is necessary for a specific purpose, rather than harvesting vast amounts of information. By reducing the amount of data collected, platforms can minimize the risks associated with data breaches and misuse.

- **Encryption and Security Measures:** Social media platforms can also protect user data by implementing strong encryption protocols and other security measures. End-to-end encryption, for example, ensures that only the sender and recipient can access the content of their messages. Platforms like WhatsApp and Signal have embraced encryption to enhance user privacy, while others are following suit to prevent unauthorized access to personal data.

- **Anonymization and Pseudonymization:** Anonymization techniques, such as stripping identifying information from user data, can help balance innovation with privacy by allowing platforms to analyse data without exposing individuals. Pseudonymization, where personal identifiers are replaced with fictitious names or numbers, can also reduce privacy risks while still enabling data-driven insights.

9.5 The Ethical Responsibility of Social Media Platforms

Beyond legal obligations, social media platforms have an ethical responsibility to protect their users' data and foster a culture of trust. Ethical considerations should guide their decision-making processes as they continue to innovate.

- **Data Ownership and User Control:** Many advocates argue that users should have full ownership and control over their personal data. This means granting users the ability to easily delete their data, export it to other platforms, and decide which companies can access it. By putting data ownership in the hands of users, platforms can empower individuals while building trust.

- **Ethical AI and Algorithm Transparency:** Social media platforms increasingly rely on artificial intelligence (AI) to personalize content and target ads. However, these AI systems often operate in opaque ways, raising concerns about bias, discrimination, and the manipulation of user behaviour. Ethical AI practices, including transparency in how algorithms function and ensuring fairness, are critical to maintaining a balance between innovation and ethical responsibility.

- **Protecting Vulnerable Populations:** Certain groups, such as children, elderly users, and individuals in politically unstable regions, may be more vulnerable to privacy violations and data misuse. Social media platforms must take additional precautions to protect these groups, offering enhanced privacy controls and implementing age-appropriate content filters where necessary.

9.6 The Future of Data Privacy on Social Media

As technology advances, the future of data privacy on social media is likely to be shaped by emerging trends and innovations. Several developments could redefine the relationship between social media platforms and data privacy:

- **Decentralized Social Media Platforms:** In response to concerns over centralized control and data privacy, decentralized social media platforms are gaining traction. These platforms, often built on blockchain technology, give users more control over their data and offer greater transparency in how information is managed. By decentralizing data ownership, these platforms could provide an alternative to traditional social media models.

- **Zero-Data Platforms:** Some platforms are experimenting with the concept of zero-data services, where no personal information is collected from users. This approach prioritizes privacy over data-driven advertising, offering users an ad-free experience without compromising their personal information. While this model challenges the current revenue streams of most social media platforms, it could represent the next frontier in privacy-centric social networks.

- **AI and Privacy-Enhancing Technologies:** Privacy-enhancing technologies, such as homomorphic encryption and differential privacy, allow platforms to process and analyse data without exposing individuals' identities. These technologies could enable social media platforms to innovate while significantly reducing privacy risks. AI systems trained to prioritize privacy could also help platforms implement smarter, more secure data management practices.

Conclusion

The relationship between social media and data privacy is complex, requiring a careful balance between innovation and the protection of personal information. While social media platforms have revolutionized communication and business, they must also prioritize user privacy to maintain trust and foster a secure digital environment. As regulations tighten and user expectations evolve, platforms will need to adopt more transparent, ethical, and secure data practices to succeed in the future.

In the next chapter, **Chapter 10: Social Media in Times of Crisis: A Tool for Resilience and Recovery**, we will explore how social media has become a crucial resource in times of crisis, from natural disasters to global pandemics, facilitating communication, coordination, and recovery efforts.

Chapter 10: Social Media and the Future of Human Interaction

In the rapidly evolving digital age, social media has fundamentally reshaped the ways we communicate, form relationships, and interact with the world around us. While it offers unprecedented opportunities for connection, it also presents new challenges, raising questions about the future of human interaction. This chapter will explore how social media is transforming communication, both personally and societally, and what the future holds for our social fabric in this increasingly digital era.

10.1 The Evolution of Communication: From Face-to-Face to Digital Interaction

Over the past few decades, communication has shifted from face-to-face interaction to digital forms, largely driven by social media platforms. These platforms have not only altered the speed and reach of communication but have also introduced new dynamics to how we engage with others.

- **Instant and Global Communication:** Social media allows for real-time communication across geographical boundaries, enabling individuals to connect with friends, family, and even strangers from around the world. This global accessibility has transformed personal relationships and fostered a sense of global citizenship, making the world feel smaller and more interconnected.

- **Asynchronous Interactions:** Unlike traditional face-to-face or phone conversations, which require both parties to be present simultaneously, social media supports asynchronous communication. This means that individuals can engage in conversations on their own time, whether through messaging, commenting, or posting. While this flexibility is convenient, it also changes the nature of conversation, often reducing the depth and immediacy of interpersonal interactions.

- **Multimodal Communication:** Social media integrates various forms of communication - text, images, videos, emojis, and GIFs - allowing users to express themselves in diverse ways. This multimodal approach to communication enhances the richness of interaction, enabling users to convey emotions and ideas in ways that go beyond words. However, it can also introduce ambiguity, as non-verbal cues are often misinterpreted or lost in digital exchanges.

10.2 The Impact of Social Media on Personal Relationships

Social media has had a profound effect on personal relationships, influencing how we build and maintain connections with others. While it offers numerous benefits for staying in touch, it also introduces complexities that affect the quality and nature of relationships.

- **Strengthening Long-Distance Relationships:** One of the most significant benefits of social media is its ability to maintain long-distance relationships. Whether through direct messaging, video calls, or shared content, social media allows individuals to stay connected with loved ones across time zones and continents. This has proven especially valuable during events like the COVID-19 pandemic, where physical separation became the norm.

- **Superficial Connections:** While social media facilitates more connections, the quality of those connections can be called into question. The ease of "friending" or "following" others often leads to a large number of superficial connections, where interactions are limited to likes, shares, or brief comments. These surface-level interactions can give the illusion of closeness without the emotional depth found in more meaningful relationships.

- **FOMO and Social Comparison:** Social media's constant stream of curated content can lead to feelings of inadequacy or "fear of missing out" (FOMO). Seeing others post about achievements, vacations, or social events may cause individuals to compare their lives to an idealized version of others, leading to dissatisfaction with their own experiences. This can strain relationships, both with oneself and with others, as people strive to present a perfect image online.

- **Shifting Dynamics in Romantic Relationships:** Social media has also influenced romantic relationships, offering both opportunities and challenges. While platforms like dating apps provide new avenues for meeting potential partners, social media can introduce complications in relationships, such as jealousy, insecurity, or blurred boundaries between public and private life. The ability to monitor a partner's online activity can sometimes lead to issues of trust and communication.

10.3 Social Media and Collective Interaction: Communities and Digital Societies

Beyond personal relationships, social media has given rise to new forms of collective interaction, where communities are built, cultures are shared, and societal norms are negotiated online.

- **Online Communities:** Social media platforms host diverse online communities where individuals with shared interests can come together.

Whether through Facebook groups, Reddit forums, or Twitter hashtags, these digital spaces foster a sense of belonging and support. For many, online communities offer validation, camaraderie, and information that may not be accessible in their physical environments.

- **Digital Activism and Civic Engagement:** Social media has also transformed how we engage with social and political causes. As discussed in earlier chapters, platforms enable individuals to organize, protest, and advocate for change on a global scale. Digital activism has reshaped civic engagement, offering a new mode of collective interaction that challenges traditional power structures. This form of interaction has made politics and social justice more accessible to those who may have previously felt disenfranchised.

- **Cultural Exchange:** Social media facilitates cross-cultural interactions, enabling individuals to learn about and engage with different cultures, perspectives, and traditions. This cultural exchange fosters greater understanding and tolerance, contributing to a more interconnected and informed global society. However, it also raises questions about cultural appropriation and the commodification of cultural practices for online consumption.

10.4 The Challenges of Social Media in Human Interaction

While social media offers immense opportunities for connection, it also presents several challenges that impact the future of human interaction. These challenges include issues related to authenticity, empathy, and the broader implications of digital reliance.

- **The Erosion of Authenticity:** The pressure to curate an idealized version of oneself on social media can lead to a disconnection from authenticity. Users may feel compelled to present a polished image that aligns with societal expectations or trends, rather than being true to themselves. This "performance" can create a disconnect between online personas and real-life identities, leading to feelings of isolation or imposter syndrome.

- **Decreased Empathy:** The digital nature of social media interactions can sometimes result in a lack of empathy. Without the physical cues that accompany face-to-face communication, such as tone, body language, and facial expressions, it is easier for misunderstandings or conflicts to arise. Moreover, the anonymity of online platforms can embolden individuals to engage in harmful behaviours, such as cyberbullying or trolling, without considering the emotional impact on others.

- **Digital Overload and Its Impact on Relationships:** As social media becomes more integrated into daily life, there is a growing concern about digital overload. Constant notifications, updates, and messages can lead to information fatigue and distract individuals from forming deeper connections. The expectation to always be available online can also strain personal relationships, as individuals struggle to balance their digital presence with real-world interactions.

10.5 Opportunities for Enriching Human Connection through Social Media

Despite the challenges, social media presents several opportunities for enriching human connection in the digital age. By leveraging the positive aspects of these platforms, we can foster deeper, more meaningful relationships and build a more inclusive and connected world.

- **Fostering Empathy and Understanding:** While social media has the potential to decrease empathy, it also offers opportunities for fostering understanding. Platforms like Humans of New York, where individuals share personal stories, can cultivate empathy by giving a voice to people from all walks of life. By amplifying diverse experiences, social media can promote compassion and bridge divides between different communities.

- **Expanding Access to Support Networks:** Social media provides access to support networks that may not exist in an individual's immediate environment. Online mental health communities, for example, offer resources and support for individuals dealing with issues like depression, anxiety, or trauma. Similarly, marginalized groups can find solidarity and strength in online spaces where they are seen and heard.

- **Innovative Ways to Build Relationships:** Social media has introduced innovative ways to build and maintain relationships. Platforms like TikTok or Clubhouse offer interactive formats that encourage creativity, participation, and engagement. These platforms have redefined how people meet, collaborate, and share experiences, offering fresh avenues for forming genuine connections.

- **Augmented and Virtual Reality:** The future of social media may also include the integration of augmented reality (AR) and virtual reality (VR). These technologies have the potential to revolutionize human interaction by creating immersive digital experiences that mimic face-to-face communication. VR social platforms like AltspaceVR or Horizon Worlds enable users to interact in virtual environments, offering new possibilities for collaboration, socialization, and even education. As these technologies advance, they could blur the lines between digital and physical worlds, creating more seamless and engaging forms of interaction.

10.6 The Future of Human Interaction in the Age of Social Media

As social media continues to evolve, the future of human interaction will be shaped by emerging trends, technologies, and societal shifts. The digital landscape is likely to become even more integrated into our daily lives, making it essential to consider how we can harness its potential while mitigating its challenges.

- **Hybrid Communication Models:** The future may see a hybrid model of communication, where digital and face-to-face interactions complement each other. Rather than replacing in-person relationships, social media can enhance and support them, offering new ways to stay connected in an increasingly busy and globalized world.

- **Digital Literacy and Emotional Intelligence:** As social media becomes more central to human interaction, there will be a growing need for digital literacy and emotional intelligence. Understanding how to navigate online spaces, communicate effectively, and manage digital relationships will be critical skills for future generations. Educational initiatives focused on digital etiquette, empathy, and media literacy can help individuals foster healthier, more meaningful connections online.

- **Redefining Community and Belonging:** Social media will continue to redefine what it means to be part of a community. Digital spaces will become more inclusive and diverse, allowing individuals to create and join communities that reflect their unique identities and interests. As these online communities grow, they will play a significant role in shaping cultural norms, values, and collective action in the years to come.

Conclusion

Social media has radically transformed how we interact with each other, offering both opportunities and challenges for the future of human connection. While it has introduced new forms of communication, expanded access to communities, and fostered global relationships, it has also raised concerns about authenticity, empathy, and the quality of our interactions. As we look to the future, it is crucial to navigate these platforms thoughtfully, leveraging their potential to enrich human connection while addressing the challenges they present.

In the next chapter, **Chapter 11: The Economic Power of Social Media: From Influencers to E-Commerce**, we will examine how social media has revolutionized the economy, creating new industries, reshaping traditional businesses, and empowering individuals to monetize their online presence.

Chapter 11: The Economic Power of Social Media: From Influencers to E-Commerce

Social media has transformed from a platform for personal interaction into a powerful economic engine. It has created new industries, reshaped traditional businesses, and empowered individuals to monetize their online presence. From influencers driving consumer behaviour to the rise of social commerce, the economic power of social media continues to grow, reshaping the way we think about business, marketing, and entrepreneurship.

11.1 The Rise of the Influencer Economy

Influencers have become central figures in the social media ecosystem, leveraging their personal brands to impact consumer behaviour, marketing strategies, and even social trends. Their ability to build loyal followings and directly engage with audiences has made them valuable assets for brands across industries.

- **From Celebrities to Everyday Individuals:** While traditional celebrity endorsements have always played a role in marketing, social media influencers differ in that they can emerge from everyday individuals. Platforms like Instagram, YouTube, and TikTok allow anyone to gain prominence by creating content that resonates with specific audiences. This democratization of influence has expanded the pool of people who can shape consumer choices.

- **Trust and Authenticity:** A key factor in the rise of influencers is the trust and authenticity they build with their followers. Influencers often share personal stories, experiences, and recommendations, creating a sense of relatability that traditional advertising lacks. This perceived authenticity is what drives their economic power, as consumers are more likely to purchase products endorsed by influencers they trust.

- **Micro and Nano Influencers:** Beyond the mega-influencers with millions of followers, there has been a rise in micro-influencers (those with 10,000–100,000 followers) and nano-influencers (those with fewer than 10,000 followers). These smaller influencers often have highly engaged, niche audiences, making them valuable to brands seeking targeted marketing. Micro and nano influencers can have a more intimate connection with their followers, leading to higher engagement rates and more authentic promotional content.

11.2 Social Media Marketing: A Paradigm Shift in Advertising

Social media has revolutionized marketing by shifting the focus from traditional mass advertising to more personalized, direct, and interactive forms of promotion. Brands have adapted their strategies to leverage the unique features of social media platforms, tapping into the power of user-generated content, targeted advertising, and data-driven insights.

- **Targeted Advertising and Data Analytics:** One of the most significant advantages of social media advertising is the ability to target specific demographics with precision. Platforms like Facebook, Instagram, and LinkedIn offer businesses the ability to run ads based on user data such as age, location, interests, and online behaviour. This targeted approach increases the effectiveness of marketing campaigns and allows brands to reach audiences who are most likely to engage with their products or services.

- **User-Generated Content:** Social media allows brands to encourage user-generated content, where customers share their experiences and interactions with products. This type of content serves as a form of word-of-mouth marketing, often perceived as more credible than traditional ads. Campaigns that encourage users to share content with specific hashtags or engage in challenges (like TikTok's viral trends) can create organic buzz around a brand.

- **Real-Time Engagement and Feedback:** Social media provides businesses with the ability to interact with consumers in real time, allowing for immediate feedback and engagement. Brands can use platforms to respond to customer inquiries, address concerns, and even handle crises as they unfold. This dynamic interaction fosters stronger relationships with customers and humanizes the brand.

11.3 The Emergence of Social Commerce

Social commerce, the integration of social media and e-commerce, is rapidly transforming the retail landscape. Consumers are now able to discover, research, and purchase products directly through social media platforms, blending the convenience of online shopping with the interactive and engaging nature of social media.

- **In-App Shopping and Seamless Transactions:** Social media platforms like Instagram, Facebook, and Pinterest have introduced in-app shopping features that allow users to browse and purchase products without leaving the platform. Instagram's "Shop" feature, for instance, allows brands to tag products in posts and stories, making it easy for users to make purchases with just a few clicks. This seamless integration of commerce into social media platforms reduces friction in the buying process and encourages impulse purchases.

- **Livestream Shopping:** Livestream shopping, popularized in markets like China, is gaining traction globally through platforms like TikTok and YouTube. Livestream events allow influencers or brand representatives to showcase products in real-time, interact with viewers, and answer questions, creating a more personalized and interactive shopping experience. This format blends entertainment with e-commerce, driving engagement and sales.

- **Social Proof and Peer Influence:** Social media fosters a sense of community, and purchasing decisions are often influenced by social proof. When users see friends, influencers, or people in their networks endorsing a product, they are more likely to trust and purchase that product themselves. This peer influence drives the success of social commerce, as consumers feel validated in their decisions by the recommendations of others within their social circles.

11.4 Social Media as a Launchpad for Entrepreneurs

For entrepreneurs and small businesses, social media has become an essential tool for launching and scaling ventures. It provides a cost-effective way to build brand awareness, connect with customers, and generate sales without the need for traditional marketing infrastructure.

- **Direct-to-Consumer (D2C) Brands:** Social media has enabled the rise of direct-to-consumer (D2C) brands that bypass traditional retail channels and sell directly to customers. Platforms like Instagram and Facebook allow entrepreneurs to build brands, reach target audiences, and sell products without needing to invest in physical storefronts. The success of D2C brands like Warby Parker, Glossier, and Gymshark highlights the potential of social media as a primary sales channel.

- **Crowdfunding and Social Validation:** Social media has also transformed how entrepreneurs fund their ventures through platforms like Kickstarter or GoFundMe. These crowdfunding sites are often promoted through social media, allowing entrepreneurs to raise capital while simultaneously building an engaged community of supporters. The social validation gained through these campaigns can attract further investment and media attention, helping to propel new businesses.

- **Building Personal Brands:** Many entrepreneurs leverage social media to build personal brands that complement their business ventures. By sharing insights, thought leadership, and behind-the-scenes content, entrepreneurs can establish themselves as authorities in their fields, building trust with potential customers and partners. Platforms like LinkedIn, Twitter, and

Instagram have become key channels for personal branding, enabling entrepreneurs to differentiate themselves and gain credibility.

11.5 The Globalization of Small Business Through Social Media

Social media has broken down geographical barriers, enabling small businesses to reach global markets with ease. What once required international marketing campaigns and significant resources can now be achieved through a strong social media presence and strategic use of platforms.

- **Reaching International Audiences:** Social media allows small businesses to tap into international markets by connecting with customers from all over the world. For example, Etsy sellers, digital artists, or independent fashion brands can promote their products globally through Instagram or Pinterest. This global reach opens up new revenue streams and growth opportunities that were previously inaccessible to smaller players.

- **Cross-Cultural Marketing:** With social media's global reach comes the need for cross-cultural marketing strategies. Small businesses must be mindful of cultural differences and consumer preferences across regions. Social media platforms provide valuable data and insights that allow businesses to tailor their messaging, products, and services to specific markets, ensuring relevance and resonance.

11.6 Challenges in the Social Media Economy

While social media offers numerous economic opportunities, it also presents challenges that businesses, entrepreneurs, and consumers must navigate.

- **Platform Dependency:** Many businesses are heavily reliant on social media platforms for marketing and sales, which can be risky if platforms change their algorithms, policies, or features. A sudden change in visibility or reach can have a significant impact on a business's bottom line. Diversifying marketing strategies and building direct relationships with customers can help mitigate this risk.

- **Data Privacy and Consumer Trust:** Social media platforms often rely on user data for targeted advertising and insights, which raises concerns about privacy and data security. Businesses must be transparent about their data practices and prioritize protecting consumer information to maintain trust. Additionally, ongoing regulatory changes, such as the implementation of data privacy laws like GDPR, require businesses to adapt and ensure compliance.

- **Market Saturation and Competition:** The accessibility of social media has led to increased competition, making it harder for new businesses to stand out. In saturated markets, businesses must find creative ways to differentiate themselves and offer unique value propositions to capture and retain customers.

11.7 The Future of Social Media and the Economy

As social media continues to evolve, its economic impact will only grow, with emerging trends and technologies poised to further revolutionize how we conduct business.

- **Integration of AI and Automation:** Artificial intelligence and automation are expected to play an increasingly important role in social media marketing. AI-powered chatbots, personalized recommendations, and predictive analytics will enhance the customer experience, making interactions more efficient and tailored. Automation tools will also help businesses manage their social media presence, from scheduling posts to analysing performance metrics.

- **Blockchain and Decentralized Social Media:** Blockchain technology has the potential to disrupt traditional social media platforms by enabling decentralized networks that give users more control over their data and content. Decentralized social media platforms could create new economic models, such as cryptocurrency-based rewards for content creators, further democratizing access to monetization opportunities.

- **Virtual Reality and Immersive Commerce:** As virtual reality (VR) and augmented reality (AR) technologies advance, social media platforms may integrate immersive experiences into e-commerce. Virtual stores, interactive product demos, and 3D virtual environments will provide users with more engaging ways to shop and explore brands.

Conclusion

Social media has revolutionized the economy, providing unprecedented opportunities for businesses, entrepreneurs, and individuals to innovate, market, and monetize their presence online. From the rise of influencers to the growth of social commerce, these platforms have reshaped traditional industries and created entirely new economic landscapes. As social media continues to evolve, businesses must adapt to emerging trends and technologies, leveraging the power of these platforms to thrive in the digital economy.

In the next chapter, **Chapter 12: Social Media and Cultural Exchange: Bridging Divides and Promoting Understanding**, we will explore how social media fosters cross-cultural dialogue, challenges stereotypes, and promotes global understanding by connecting people from diverse backgrounds.

Chapter 12: Social Media and Cultural Exchange: Bridging Divides and Promoting Understanding

Social media has opened the door to unprecedented levels of cultural exchange, enabling people from diverse backgrounds to interact, share their experiences, and learn from one another. By breaking down geographical and linguistic barriers, social media fosters cross-cultural dialogue, challenges stereotypes, and promotes global understanding. In this chapter, we will explore how social media acts as a bridge between cultures, how it influences our perceptions of the world, and the challenges it presents in achieving true global harmony.

12.1 Social Media as a Platform for Cross-Cultural Dialogue

One of the most significant impacts of social media is its ability to connect individuals from different cultures, providing a platform for dialogue that might not have been possible otherwise. Through these interactions, people gain a deeper understanding of the values, traditions, and perspectives of others, fostering empathy and breaking down cultural barriers.

- **Global Connectivity and Instant Communication:** Social media platforms like Facebook, Twitter, and Instagram allow users from all over the world to engage in real-time conversations. Whether it's discussing global events, participating in online forums, or sharing personal stories, social media facilitates immediate communication that transcends borders. This global connectivity fosters the exchange of ideas and perspectives, promoting a more interconnected world.

- **Language and Translation Tools:** One of the primary obstacles to cross-cultural dialogue has historically been language. Social media platforms have increasingly integrated translation tools that enable users to communicate across linguistic barriers. Platforms like Facebook and Twitter provide automatic translation features, making it easier for users to engage with content in different languages and participate in global conversations.

- **Sharing Cultural Experiences:** Social media enables users to share their cultural practices, traditions, and experiences through photos, videos, and stories. This visual and interactive exchange allows individuals to immerse themselves in different cultures, whether by following travel influencers, engaging with international art, or learning about different cuisines and customs.

12.2 Challenging Stereotypes and Combating Cultural Misunderstanding

Cultural stereotypes and misunderstandings often arise from a lack of exposure to other cultures or from narrow representations in mainstream media. Social media provides an opportunity to challenge these stereotypes by offering more nuanced and diverse perspectives.

- **Amplifying Authentic Voices:** Social media allows individuals from marginalized or underrepresented cultures to share their stories and experiences directly with global audiences, bypassing traditional media gatekeepers. By sharing their own narratives, these individuals can offer a more accurate and authentic portrayal of their cultures, helping to dismantle stereotypes and counteract misconceptions.

- **Educational Campaigns and Initiatives:** Social media has become a powerful tool for educational campaigns that aim to combat prejudice, discrimination, and cultural ignorance. Organizations and influencers can use platforms to spread awareness about social issues, historical events, and cultural practices, promoting tolerance and understanding. For example, campaigns like "Humans of New York" highlight personal stories from people across different backgrounds, fostering empathy and challenging preconceived notions.

- **Cultural Exchange Programs and Virtual Travel:** Social media platforms have also facilitated virtual cultural exchange programs, where users from different countries can participate in discussions, share media, and learn about each other's cultures in an organized manner. Virtual travel experiences have emerged as well, allowing people to explore different parts of the world through social media, thus reducing cultural ignorance and broadening perspectives.

12.3 Promoting Global Understanding Through Shared Experiences

Social media has the power to create shared global experiences, fostering a sense of unity and promoting mutual understanding. Whether through global events, viral movements, or collaborative efforts, people from diverse backgrounds come together around common causes, promoting a shared sense of humanity.

- **Global Events and Solidarity:** When significant global events occur, such as natural disasters, political upheavals, or international celebrations, social media becomes a platform for solidarity and collective action. For example, the outpouring of support after major disasters—like earthquakes or wildfires—shows how social media can unite people in offering aid and raising awareness, regardless of their cultural backgrounds.

- **Cultural Celebrations and Festivals:** Social media also plays a crucial role in promoting global participation in cultural celebrations and festivals. From Chinese New Year to Diwali, Ramadan to Christmas, users around the world share their experiences, rituals, and customs. These celebrations help create a more inclusive digital environment where individuals can appreciate and participate in the cultural events of others.

- **Shared Artistic and Creative Expression:** Art, music, and storytelling are universal languages that transcend cultural boundaries. Social media provides a platform for artists, musicians, and creators from different cultures to collaborate and share their work with global audiences. Collaborative art projects, viral dance challenges, and international music exchanges are just a few examples of how social media encourages creative cultural fusion.

12.4 Challenges in Fostering True Cultural Understanding

While social media has made significant strides in bridging cultural divides, challenges remain in achieving genuine global understanding. Miscommunication, cultural appropriation, and the spread of misinformation can sometimes undermine the positive potential of social media as a tool for cultural exchange.

- **Cultural Appropriation:** One of the most contentious issues arising from global cultural exchanges on social media is cultural appropriation—the adoption of elements of one culture by another, often without proper understanding or respect. While some exchanges are done in appreciation, others can be perceived as exploitation, particularly when dominant cultures appropriate symbols, clothing, or rituals from marginalized cultures. Social media has become a space where these conversations take place, with activists and communities calling for greater respect and understanding of cultural boundaries.

- **Echo Chambers and Filter Bubbles:** Social media algorithms often promote content based on user preferences, which can create echo chambers where users are exposed only to ideas and perspectives they already agree with. This can reinforce stereotypes and prevent meaningful cross-cultural dialogue. While social media has the potential to broaden horizons, users must actively seek out diverse viewpoints to overcome these algorithmic barriers.

- **Misinformation and Cultural Misrepresentation:** The rapid spread of misinformation on social media can lead to cultural misrepresentation and perpetuate harmful stereotypes. False or sensationalized portrayals of certain

103

cultures can spread quickly, influencing public perceptions. Combating this challenge requires users to critically evaluate the content they consume and share, as well as a collective effort to promote accurate, informed depictions of cultural practices.

12.5 The Future of Social Media and Cultural Exchange

As social media continues to evolve, its role in facilitating cultural exchange will likely expand, offering new opportunities for connection and understanding.

- **Virtual and Augmented Reality Experiences:** The future of cultural exchange on social media may be enhanced through virtual reality (VR) and augmented reality (AR) technologies. These immersive experiences could allow users to explore different cultures in more interactive and engaging ways, such as taking virtual tours of historical landmarks, participating in virtual festivals, or learning languages through immersive simulations.

- **AI and Language Barriers:** Advances in artificial intelligence (AI) could further break down language barriers by offering more accurate real-time translation tools. These technologies could facilitate even more seamless communication between people from different cultures, enabling deeper conversations and connections.

- **Decentralized Platforms for Cultural Exchange:** Emerging technologies like blockchain may lead to decentralized social media platforms that empower users to create content and interact without the influence of large corporations. These platforms could encourage more authentic and respectful cultural exchanges, as users retain control over their data and content.

Conclusion

Social media has emerged as a powerful tool for cultural exchange, enabling individuals from diverse backgrounds to engage in dialogue, share their experiences, and challenge stereotypes. By fostering global connections, amplifying authentic voices, and promoting shared experiences, social media has the potential to create a more interconnected and understanding world. However, it is essential to navigate the challenges of cultural appropriation, misinformation, and echo chambers to realize the full potential of social media as a bridge between cultures.

In the next chapter, **Chapter 13: Social Media and Civic Engagement: Empowering Citizens and Strengthening Democracies**, we will explore how social media is shaping civic participation, empowering citizens, and contributing to the strengthening - or weakening - of democratic processes across the globe.

Chapter 13: Social Media and Civic Engagement: Empowering Citizens and Strengthening Democracies

Social media has revolutionized civic engagement by providing a platform for citizens to participate in political discourse, access information, and mobilize for social change. In this chapter, we will explore how social media empowers individuals, influences political participation, and plays a complex role in shaping democratic processes. While social media offers unprecedented opportunities for engagement, it also presents challenges, such as misinformation, polarization, and the manipulation of public opinion.

13.1 Social Media as a Tool for Civic Empowerment

Social media provides citizens with an accessible, immediate, and interactive platform for engaging with political and civic issues. Through social media, individuals can express their opinions, participate in debates, and mobilize around causes that matter to them.

- **Direct Access to Information:** Social media platforms like Twitter, Facebook, and Instagram serve as major sources of news and political updates. Users can follow politicians, public figures, and media outlets, receiving direct and real-time access to political events, policies, and government actions. This democratization of information makes it easier for citizens to stay informed, especially when traditional media sources may be inaccessible or limited.

- **Amplifying Marginalized Voices:** Social media provides a space for underrepresented and marginalized groups to voice their concerns and share their perspectives. In countries where access to mainstream media may be restricted or biased, social media becomes a tool for political resistance, helping marginalized communities advocate for their rights and influence the political agenda.

- **Facilitating Grassroots Mobilization:** Social media enables grassroots organizations and activists to organize campaigns, protests, and movements. By leveraging social networks, these groups can quickly mobilize supporters, raise awareness, and coordinate events. The viral nature of social media means that even small-scale initiatives can reach a global audience, gaining momentum and attracting widespread attention.

13.2 Case Studies: Social Media-Driven Civic Movements

Over the last decade, several high-profile civic movements have demonstrated the power of social media in organizing, mobilizing, and driving political change. These case studies highlight both the strengths and limitations of social media in shaping civic engagement.

- **Arab Spring (2010-2012):** The Arab Spring was a series of anti-government protests across the Middle East and North Africa, fuelled in part by social media. Activists used platforms like Facebook and Twitter to coordinate protests, share information about government crackdowns, and communicate with the global community. Social media allowed for the rapid dissemination of ideas, enabling citizens to challenge authoritarian regimes. However, the role of social media was double-edged, as it also led to government surveillance and the suppression of activists.

- **Hong Kong Protests (2019-2020):** The pro-democracy protests in Hong Kong showcased how social media can be used to organize large-scale demonstrations. Platforms like Telegram, Instagram, and Twitter were used to coordinate protest actions, share live updates, and spread awareness about police violence. The decentralized nature of social media allowed protesters to evade government censorship and organize anonymously, demonstrating how social media can empower civic action even in restrictive environments.

- **Youth-Led Movements (Global):** Social media has played a significant role in amplifying the voices of young activists across the globe, from Greta Thunberg's climate activism to the #MarchForOurLives movement against gun violence in the U.S. These movements have demonstrated the ability of social media to connect young people, spark global conversations, and influence political discourse. Social media platforms offer youth a direct channel to engage with politicians, challenge the status quo, and advocate for policy change.

13.3 The Role of Social Media in Elections and Political Campaigning

Social media has fundamentally transformed how political campaigns are run, enabling candidates to communicate directly with voters, fundraise, and mobilize support. However, its role in elections also raises important questions about transparency, misinformation, and influence.

- **Direct Voter Engagement:** Political candidates and parties increasingly rely on social media to engage with voters, bypassing traditional media outlets. Platforms like Twitter and Facebook allow politicians to deliver campaign messages, interact with constituents, and respond to political developments in real-time. This direct engagement fosters a sense of connection between politicians and the public, making the political process feel more accessible.

- **Fundraising and Crowdsourcing:** Social media enables political campaigns to raise funds through small, grassroots donations. Platforms like GoFundMe and crowdfunding sites have allowed candidates, especially those from underfunded parties, to generate substantial financial support from individual donors. This has democratized the political funding landscape and made it possible for more diverse candidates to run for office.

- **Micro-Targeting and Political Ads:** Social media platforms have transformed how political advertising is conducted, using data-driven micro-targeting to deliver personalized ads to users. While this can be an effective way to reach specific voter demographics, it has also raised concerns about privacy, transparency, and the potential for manipulation. Political ads on platforms like Facebook have been scrutinized for spreading misinformation and contributing to political polarization.

13.4 Challenges: Misinformation, Polarization, and Algorithmic Influence

While social media has created new avenues for political engagement, it also presents significant challenges that can undermine democratic processes.

- **Misinformation and Fake News:** The rapid spread of misinformation on social media is one of the most pressing challenges to civic engagement. False or misleading information, often amplified by algorithms, can shape public opinion and influence political outcomes. During elections, social media has been used to spread disinformation campaigns, leading to voter confusion and distrust in the electoral process. Combatting misinformation requires greater media literacy and efforts by platforms to regulate harmful content.

- **Polarization and Echo Chambers:** Social media algorithms often prioritize content that aligns with users' existing beliefs, creating "echo chambers" where individuals are exposed only to ideas that reinforce their views. This can deepen political divisions, increase polarization, and reduce opportunities for constructive dialogue. As a result, social media can sometimes contribute to a more fragmented and less civil political landscape.

- **Manipulation and Interference:** Foreign interference in elections through social media manipulation has raised concerns about the integrity of democratic processes. Disinformation campaigns, bot networks, and the spread of divisive content by external actors have been documented in several high-profile elections, including the 2016 U.S. presidential election and the Brexit referendum. Social media platforms have been called upon to implement stronger measures to prevent external manipulation and ensure fair political engagement.

13.5 The Future of Social Media and Civic Engagement

As social media continues to evolve, its role in civic engagement will likely become even more complex. Emerging technologies, regulatory changes, and new platforms will shape the future of political participation in the digital age.

- **Blockchain and Decentralized Platforms:** The emergence of blockchain technology and decentralized social media platforms may offer new ways to engage in political discourse without centralized control. These platforms could provide greater transparency and reduce the influence of algorithms, giving users more control over their online interactions. Decentralized platforms may also offer greater security and privacy for activists and marginalized groups.

- **Artificial Intelligence and Content Moderation:** As artificial intelligence (AI) advances, social media platforms will increasingly rely on AI-driven tools to moderate content, detect misinformation, and prevent the spread of harmful political content. However, this raises important questions about free speech, bias, and the role of technology in shaping political discourse.

- **Civic Engagement Tools:** Social media platforms may develop new features and tools specifically designed to facilitate civic engagement. For example, Facebook has experimented with voter registration tools, while Twitter has partnered with NGOs to promote civic participation. These features could make it easier for citizens to engage with political processes and access accurate information about elections and policies.

Conclusion

Social media has transformed civic engagement, empowering citizens to participate in political discourse, organize grassroots movements, and hold institutions accountable. However, it has also introduced new challenges, such as misinformation, polarization, and external manipulation. As we look to the future, it is essential to recognize both the opportunities and risks of social media in shaping democratic processes and to work towards creating a more informed, inclusive, and responsible digital political sphere.

In the next chapter, **Chapter 14: Social Media and the Environment: Mobilizing for Sustainability and Climate Action**, we will explore how social media is being used to raise awareness about environmental issues, mobilize climate activists, and promote sustainable practices across the globe.

Chapter 14: Social Media and the Environment: Mobilizing for Sustainability and Climate Action

Social media has emerged as a powerful tool in the fight against climate change and environmental degradation. It provides a platform for raising awareness about pressing environmental issues, mobilizing activists, and promoting sustainable practices. This chapter explores how social media facilitates global conversations on environmental topics, empowers individuals and organizations to take action, and shapes public opinion about sustainability. From grassroots movements to corporate responsibility campaigns, social media is playing a pivotal role in the pursuit of a more sustainable future.

14.1 Raising Awareness About Environmental Issues

One of the most significant contributions of social media to environmental advocacy is its ability to raise awareness about global environmental challenges. Social media platforms have enabled the widespread dissemination of information about issues such as climate change, deforestation, pollution, and biodiversity loss. This has led to a broader public understanding of environmental crises and encouraged greater engagement with sustainability.

- **Widespread Accessibility:** Social media makes it easy for environmental organizations, activists, and everyday users to share information and educational content. Documentaries, articles, infographics, and real-time footage of environmental disasters can be circulated instantly across platforms like Twitter, Instagram, and Facebook, reaching millions of people in seconds. This accessibility breaks down barriers to information and empowers people to educate themselves about environmental issues.

- **Viral Campaigns:** Hashtags such as #ClimateChange, #SaveThePlanet, and #FridaysForFuture have gone viral on social media, encouraging users to join global movements and take action. These viral campaigns bring environmental concerns to the forefront of public consciousness, generating conversation and sparking collective action. By using these hashtags, individuals amplify the message and contribute to greater environmental awareness.

- **Influencers and Thought Leaders:** Environmental influencers, scientists, and activists have used social media to build large followings and drive awareness around sustainability. Influencers like Greta Thunberg, Leonardo DiCaprio, and activists from organizations such as Greenpeace have leveraged their platforms to educate and inspire action. Their social media presence gives visibility to environmental issues that may otherwise be overlooked by traditional media.

14.2 Mobilizing Climate Activists and Movements

Social media has proven to be a key organizing tool for environmental movements, allowing activists to mobilize supporters, coordinate protests, and promote grassroots campaigns. It provides a decentralized and fast-moving platform for collective action.

- **Global Climate Strikes and Fridays for Future:** One of the most prominent examples of social media's role in environmental activism is the rise of the **Fridays for Future** movement, led by climate activist Greta Thunberg. What began as a solo climate strike in Sweden rapidly grew into a global movement, with millions of young people participating in climate strikes across the world. Social media played a crucial role in organizing these strikes, coordinating efforts across countries, and amplifying the movement's message to a global audience. Hashtags like #FridaysForFuture and #ClimateStrike were used to unify participants and spread awareness about strike dates and locations.

- **Grassroots Activism:** Social media has empowered grassroots environmental movements in ways that were previously unimaginable. Local and community-based organizations can now coordinate and collaborate on a global scale, sharing strategies, tactics, and resources. For example, campaigns against deforestation, plastic pollution, and fossil fuel extraction have benefited from the connectivity that social media offers. Activists can spread their messages, garner international support, and put pressure on corporations and governments by bringing attention to their causes.

- **Digital Advocacy Tools:** Platforms like Facebook, Instagram, and Twitter provide digital advocacy tools such as petitions, crowdfunding, and event coordination. Activists can use these tools to fundraise for environmental causes, petition governments for policy changes, and organize virtual or in-person protests. For example, social media-based petitions against single-use plastics or endangered species have garnered millions of signatures, prompting corporations to change practices or governments to adopt new regulations.

14.3 Corporate Responsibility and Sustainability Campaigns

Beyond grassroots activism, social media has become an important platform for corporations to promote their sustainability initiatives and respond to public demand for environmental responsibility.

- **Corporate Green Initiatives:** Many companies have embraced social media to showcase their commitment to environmental sustainability. From reducing carbon emissions to adopting circular economy practices, businesses use platforms like LinkedIn and Instagram to communicate their environmental goals and achievements. Social media allows them to highlight their green initiatives, build brand loyalty among environmentally conscious consumers, and provide transparency regarding their sustainability efforts.

- **Consumer Pressure and Accountability:** Social media has made it easier for consumers to hold corporations accountable for their environmental practices. Users frequently share their concerns about corporate behaviour, encouraging more sustainable business models through collective pressure. When companies engage in environmentally harmful practices, they often face backlash on social media, leading to public relations challenges and calls for change. For example, fashion brands involved in fast fashion or tech companies producing excessive e-waste have faced public scrutiny on platforms like Twitter.

- **Influence of Eco-Friendly Brands and Products:** Social media has also contributed to the rise of eco-friendly brands and products, as consumers seek out companies that prioritize sustainability. Platforms like Instagram and Pinterest feature influencers and brands promoting sustainable fashion, zero-waste lifestyles, and eco-friendly products. Social media has made it easier for consumers to discover green products, learn about sustainable practices, and make purchasing decisions that align with their environmental values.

14.4 Educating and Inspiring Sustainable Lifestyles

In addition to raising awareness and driving activism, social media also plays a role in educating individuals about how to live more sustainably. It encourages the adoption of environmentally conscious practices, from reducing plastic use to lowering one's carbon footprint.

- **Sustainability Influencers:** A growing number of influencers focus on promoting sustainable lifestyles. These individuals use platforms like YouTube, Instagram, and TikTok to share tips on reducing waste, adopting plant-based diets, and making eco-friendly choices in everyday life. By making sustainability more relatable and accessible, these influencers inspire their followers to take small, meaningful actions.

- **DIY and Upcycling Communities:** Social media fosters communities that promote DIY (do-it-yourself) and upcycling practices. Platforms like Pinterest and YouTube are filled with tutorials on how to repurpose old items, reduce waste, and create environmentally friendly products at home. These communities encourage creativity and resourcefulness, helping people reduce their consumption and contribute to a circular economy.

- **Climate Education Resources:** Social media platforms also provide access to a wealth of climate education resources. NGOs, educators, and scientists use platforms like Twitter and LinkedIn to share research, climate reports, and actionable strategies for addressing environmental challenges. This democratization of knowledge allows individuals to better understand the science of climate change and participate in informed discussions.

14.5 Challenges of Social Media for Environmental Advocacy

While social media is a powerful tool for environmental advocacy, it is not without its challenges. These challenges include misinformation, superficial activism, and the environmental impact of digital platforms themselves.

- **Misinformation and Greenwashing:** As with other social issues, misinformation can spread quickly on social media platforms, making it difficult for users to discern accurate information about environmental topics. Furthermore, some corporations engage in "greenwashing," where they falsely claim to be environmentally responsible without taking meaningful action. This creates confusion and undermines the credibility of legitimate sustainability efforts.

- **Superficial Activism ("Slacktivism"):** While social media can drive powerful movements, it can also foster superficial forms of activism, often referred to as "slacktivism." This occurs when users engage with environmental causes by liking, sharing, or commenting on posts without taking any concrete action. While social media can raise awareness, it is essential that digital engagement translates into real-world activism and policy change.

- **The Environmental Cost of Digital Platforms:** Paradoxically, the technology that powers social media platforms has an environmental impact of its own. Data centres, which store the vast amounts of information shared on social media, consume significant amounts of energy and contribute to carbon emissions. The production and disposal of electronic devices used to access social media platforms also have an environmental footprint. These factors raise important questions about the sustainability of the digital infrastructure behind social media.

14.6 The Future of Social Media and Environmental Advocacy

Looking ahead, social media is likely to play an even more prominent role in the fight for environmental sustainability. Emerging technologies, new platforms, and increasing public awareness will continue to shape the future of environmental advocacy.

- **Virtual and Augmented Reality for Environmental Awareness:** The rise of virtual and augmented reality (VR/AR) technologies may enhance how people engage with environmental issues. Immersive experiences, such as virtual tours of endangered ecosystems or simulations of climate change impacts, could help people better understand the urgency of environmental challenges.

- **AI-Powered Environmental Solutions:** Artificial intelligence (AI) and data analytics are being integrated into social media platforms to monitor environmental trends, track sustainability goals, and analyse the impact of advocacy efforts. AI tools could help organizations optimize their campaigns, better understand public sentiment, and identify emerging environmental threats.

- **Collaborative Global Movements:** As social media continues to connect people across the globe, we can expect to see more collaborative, international movements pushing for systemic environmental change. Global networks of activists, scientists, and policymakers will increasingly leverage social media to coordinate efforts, share knowledge, and advocate for policy reform.

Conclusion

Social media has become a central force in the environmental movement, enabling widespread awareness, mobilizing activists, and encouraging sustainable practices. By connecting individuals, fostering global conversations, and holding corporations accountable, social media is reshaping how we address environmental issues. While there are challenges to navigate, such as misinformation and greenwashing, the potential for social media to drive meaningful environmental action is undeniable. As we move into an era of greater digital connectivity, it is crucial to harness the power of social media for the long-term health of our planet.

In the next chapter, **Chapter 15: Conclusion: Social Media as a Transformative Force for Good**, we will summarize the key themes of the book and reflect on the overall impact of social media on society, culture, and the future.

Chapter 15: Conclusion: Social Media as a Transformative Force for Good

As we conclude this exploration of social media's impact on society, it is clear that social media has become a transformative force, reshaping the way we communicate, engage, and understand the world around us. Despite its complexities and challenges, the overall potential of social media to create positive change is vast. In this chapter, we will summarize the key themes discussed throughout the book and reflect on how social media has revolutionized society, while considering its future implications.

15.1 Revolutionizing Communication and Global Connectivity

Social media has revolutionized communication, breaking down geographic, cultural, and linguistic barriers to create a more connected world. It allows individuals and groups to communicate instantaneously, sharing ideas, stories, and experiences across borders. This has transformed how we build relationships, stay informed, and engage with global issues.

- **Global Connectivity:** The ability to connect with anyone, anywhere, at any time has fostered a sense of global citizenship, enabling us to develop deeper empathy and understanding of diverse perspectives.

- **Instantaneous Communication:** Real-time interaction has changed everything from personal conversations to global business operations, ensuring that people and information are more accessible than ever before.

15.2 Amplifying Voices and Supporting Social Movements

Social media has become a critical platform for amplifying marginalized voices and supporting social justice movements. It provides a space where individuals, regardless of background, can raise awareness about issues, organize for change, and hold institutions accountable.

- **Empowerment of Marginalized Groups:** By offering a platform for sharing experiences and rallying around causes, social media has given power to individuals and communities traditionally excluded from mainstream discourse.

- **Grassroots Movements:** From the #MeToo movement to Black Lives Matter, social media has played a vital role in mobilizing grassroots activism and shaping public opinion on social justice issues.

15.3 Transforming Business and Economic Innovation

The rise of social media has also revolutionized business practices and created new opportunities for entrepreneurship and economic growth. It has reshaped how companies interact with consumers, market their products, and innovate in an increasingly digital economy.

- **E-Commerce and Influencers:** Social media has opened up new revenue streams through influencer marketing, brand collaborations, and e-

125

commerce integration, allowing businesses to reach audiences directly and individuals to monetize their online presence.

- **Entrepreneurship:** Social media has lowered the barrier to entry for entrepreneurs, giving them access to global markets, tools for branding, and the ability to build communities around their products or services.

15.4 Fostering Education, Cultural Exchange, and Community Building

Social media has transformed the landscape of education and cultural exchange, providing unprecedented access to information and fostering communities around shared interests. Whether enhancing formal education or facilitating informal learning, social media serves as a powerful tool for knowledge-sharing and collaboration.

- **Educational Innovation:** Platforms like YouTube and LinkedIn have become valuable educational tools, democratizing learning and professional development opportunities.

- **Cultural Exchange:** By connecting people across different cultures and backgrounds, social media helps bridge divides, challenge stereotypes, and promote global understanding.

15.5 The Double-Edged Sword: Mental Health and Civic Engagement

While social media offers numerous benefits, it is also essential to recognize its potential downsides. The relationship between social media and mental health is complex, as its constant connectivity can lead to both positive and negative emotional outcomes. Moreover, while social media enhances civic engagement, it can also contribute to the spread of misinformation and political polarization.

- **Mental Health Considerations:** Social media can foster connection, support, and community, but it can also exacerbate anxiety, depression, and loneliness if not used mindfully.

- **Political Engagement:** Social media has empowered citizens to engage with political processes, but it also poses challenges to informed, civil discourse, as echo chambers and disinformation spread easily.

15.6 Shaping the Future of Human Interaction

As we move further into the digital age, social media will continue to shape the future of human interaction. Its influence on how we form relationships, build communities, and communicate will only deepen, offering new opportunities while also presenting fresh challenges.

- **Technological Integration:** Emerging technologies, such as artificial intelligence, virtual reality, and blockchain, will further integrate with social media platforms, offering new possibilities for engagement and interaction.

- **Human Connection:** While there are concerns about the erosion of face-to-face communication, social media offers tools to enhance our connections, foster collaboration, and promote a more inclusive global society.

15.7 Balancing Innovation with Privacy and Ethics

One of the major challenges moving forward will be finding a balance between the innovations social media enables and the privacy concerns it raises. As users continue to share vast amounts of personal data, ensuring data security and ethical use of that information will be paramount.

- **Data Privacy:** Striking a balance between personalization and data protection will be key to maintaining user trust in social media platforms.

- **Ethical Innovation:** As social media platforms grow in complexity and reach, they will need to embrace ethical practices, ensuring that technological advancement does not come at the cost of user safety and rights.

15.8 Conclusion: Social Media's Transformative Power

Throughout this book, we have explored the multifaceted impact of social media across a wide range of domains. From revolutionizing communication to empowering social movements and transforming business, social media is undeniably a powerful force for good. It has amplified voices that may otherwise go unheard, reshaped industries, and connected the world in ways once unimaginable.

However, like any tool, its impact depends on how it is used. The future of social media lies in harnessing its potential for positive change while addressing the challenges that come with it - whether that be mental health, political polarization, or data privacy. As we continue to navigate this digital landscape, we must strive to ensure that social media remains a tool for progress, inclusion, and innovation.

As we look to the future, social media's role in society will only grow. By understanding its transformative power and addressing its complexities, we can shape a future where social media continues to empower individuals, strengthen communities, and drive global progress.

The journey of social media has only just begun, and its potential to foster positive change remains vast.

www.ingramcontent.com/pod-product-compliance
Lightning Source LLC
LaVergne TN
LVHW081530050326
832903LV00025B/1712